LP

The LogicPrep Guide to Grammar

LogicPrep

About This Book

This book is the culmination of many hours of diligent work by the following people: Jamie Kenyon, Jesse Kolber, Alyssa Loh, Helen Moss, John Powers, Molly Pickel, Dan Turkel, and David Zellnik. Our dynamic team collectively has over 30 years in the test-prep industry and 20,000 hours of preparing students for both the ACT and SAT. The ordering of the lessons in this book is alphabetical, but the number of questions in each section is directly proportional to how frequently these topics are tested on the ACT and SAT. If you commit to learning the information in this book, then your performance will improve greatly.

Published by LogicPrep Tutoring, 2017
ISBN: 978-0-9851060-2-7

A Note from LogicPrep

Hi there. Welcome to the high-stakes, much-dreaded, your-whole-life-seems-to-hang-in-the-balance world of college entry exams.

Here's the good news:

If you're reading this book, you're already smart – not because you chose our book (well, not *just* because), but because you've realized that the best way to get the ACT or SAT score that you want is to prepare. Prepare logically, even.

To be sure, your ACT or SAT score will be only a part of your entire college application. Your grades, extracurriculars, outside activities, volunteer work, and of course your main essay and supplements will all factor in. But let's be honest: your test scores *will* be a big part of your application.

How did this come to be, you ask? Why are there standardized tests like the ACT and SAT in the first place? There are many reasons, but the biggest one is basically that the American education system is set up on a district-by-district basis – so colleges need a uniform national standard to find out how much you know and where you fit in with your peers. Thus, the ACT and the SAT test how much you know (of what the test-makers deem important, that is) and where your score fits in on a national bell curve. Simple, right?

This book is organized to teach you clearly and thoroughly the primary skills you'll need to ace the grammar- and rhetoric-based portions of the ACT (the English Section) and the SAT (the Writing & Language Section).

STEP 1: SKILLS

To do well on these writing-focused multiple choice sections, which are one of four multiple choice sections on the test (whether you choose the ACT or SAT), you'll need to master the following skill sets and learn how they are actually tested:

- **Grammar** - We'll review all the grammar rules you need for English: nouns and verbs and modifiers and lots of punctuation. We'll make sure that the grammar you *sort of* know becomes the grammar you *totally* know, and that you can see how these rules apply to the questions that the ACT and SAT ask.
- **Rhetoric** - Rhetoric is a fancy way of describing the questions that ask about style and organization. What is the best order of the paragraphs? Should a particular sentence be added or deleted? If the author intends to do X, which answer best accomplishes it? We'll help you see inside these questions and how to spot the correct answer.

So master these skill sets and you should be golden, right?

And yet…

STEP 2: SKILLS IN ACTION

In order to maximize your score, you need to learn how the ACT and SAT apply and test the skills you've mastered. And, even more importantly, you need – through thorough reflection and rigorous reflection – to learn how *you* best take the test.

Look, we're not in the testing room with you, but we will offer you our wisdom, honed from years of working with all different kinds of students, so we can alert you to common (and sometimes not-so-common) mistakes… and some variations on test-taking strategy so that you can find what works best for *you*.

Finally, after you've done the hard work of learning the grammar and rhetoric skills and the hard work of identifying what strategies help you the most on the ACT or SAT, there are three more skills (which may not sound like skills) that you'll need to master: being confident, being calm, and being careful.

- **BE CONFIDENT** - You have learned the knowledge you need and have seen how the ACT and SAT test it, so be strong! Neither the ACT nor the SAT varies much from test to test.
- **BE CALM** - Becoming emotional on these tests will work against you. Whether you feel you are performing well or not, you must stay calm instead of becoming excited or nervous.
- **BE CAREFUL** - Even experienced test-takers can be sloppy, or can misread a question, or can forget to plug an answer choice into the *whole* sentence… and so they let themselves get caught off-guard by a well-written but incorrect answer choice.

The road to success will be a little different for everyone, and the exact final destinations will vary, too. But here's the promise we make:

If you work hard to learn the skills we teach, and if you practice and adjust your test-taking skills, your score will improve – often by a lot. How much improvement you attain depends on *you*: on *your* hard work and on *your* commitment.

Lastly, we do teach these skill sets so you can do great on the ACT and SAT, but we wouldn't be in this business if we didn't also believe we were teaching you things that would be vital for the rest of your life. After all, writing cogently and using correct grammar are hugely important, no matter what you choose to do (and are rare enough skills that your mastery of them will give you a real leg up)! Likewise, synthesizing written information and grasping a speaker or writer's intent will help you greatly in college, in job interviews, and in, well, everything.

So jump in. The water's fine. Have some fun and know you are making an investment that will pay off – on the ACT and SAT, and beyond!

– The LogicPrep Team

Contents

Introducing the ACT English 1

Adjectives and Adverbs 7

Clarity 11

Comparative and Superlative 22

Idioms 26

Misplaced Modification 34

Noun/Pronoun Agreement 41

Organization 47

Parallelism 54

Possessives 58

Punctuation 67

Redundancy 98

Transition Words 110

Verbs: Tense and Subject Agreement 122

Writing Strategy 136

Word Choice/Vocab 160

Answer Key 163

The ACT Essay 166

Introducing the Key Grammar Concepts of the ACT and SAT

The following concepts are the ones that are most-frequently tested in the ACT English and the SAT Writing & Language section. Each of these test sections consists of passages with underlined phrases that you'll be asked to edit (or not) based on grammatical accuracy or rhetorical skills. Take a look at the concepts below to get started, then try the practice questions in the corresponding problem sets to get a more complete understanding.

Punctuation

Rule 1: If a comma is followed by a conjunction (For, And, Nor, But, Or, Yet, So; or FANBOYS), it must separate two clauses that could be sentences on their own.

> *Example*: I find Lady Gaga's act unoriginal, so I don't purchase her music.

> **Note**: The only exception to this rule, known as the Oxford comma, is considered a style choice. The Oxford comma occurs when a comma is used before 'and' at the end of a list of 3 or more things.
>
> *Example*: I recently traveled to Malaysia, Singapore, and Hong Kong.

Rule 2: Do not use commas next to prepositions.

> *Example*: The release of a recent study from the Pew Research Center demonstrated that Americans are eating less healthily than 20 years ago.

Rule 3: When giving two descriptions or titles, you must choose between using a comma and using a linking word like and, or, or but.

> *Example*: The large but overcrowded restaurant provided an awkward space for a lunchtime business meeting.
>
> OR
>
> *Example*: The large, overcrowded restaurant provided an awkward space for a lunchtime business meeting.

Rule 4: A comma is used when setting off introductory or background elements.

> *Example*: On our way to the concert, we stopped to eat dinner at a Mexican restaurant.

Rule 5: Use a comma to set off phrases that express contrast (other than but).

Example: Some people believe yawning is related to sleep. However, the real cause of yawning is still undetermined.

Rule 6: Never use only one comma between a subject and its verb (only use two or zero).

Example: Miley Cyrus, singer and actress, made a fool of herself at the MTV Video Music Awards.

OR

Example: Singer and actress Miley Cyrus made a fool of herself at the MTV Video Music Awards.

Rule 7: That and which both introduce a description of an object, but which uses commas while that does not. Who introduces a description of a person, when presents a time, and where indicates a place (these can be used with or without commas).

Example: The game, which was won by the Yankees, lasted over four hours.

OR

Example: The game that was won by the Yankees lasted over four hours.

Rule 8: The period(.) and the semicolon (;) are the same thing. So when two answer choices are the same except for a period or a semicolon, neither of them is correct.

Example: "I had a sandwich. It was tasty." is the same as "I had a sandwich; it was tasty."

Rule 9: A colon (:) is correctly used if the sentence meets 3 requirements:
1. There must be a full sentence before the colon
2. There must be no linking word next to the colon
3. The second part must somehow explain the first

Example: I like to play a variety of sports: basketball, baseball, tennis, and golf.

Rule 10: An em dash (–) is used in informal writing and occasionally in formal writing to replace a comma, semicolon, or colon. On the ACT, the em dash is used most frequently in the same way as a comma or commas.

Example: The Second Edition of the Oxford English Dictionary – considered one of the most comprehensive dictionaries – features full entries for 171,476 words in current use and 7,156 obsolete words.

Verbs

When answer choices are verbs, you must find the subject and check the tense. Verbs are action words, or forms of the word "to be." Remember that is, are, was, and were are all verbs!

Finding Subjects: The subject will always come before any prepositions (linking words such as of, by, on, around, to, etc.).

> *Examples*: (subjects in **bold**, verbs <u>underlined</u>, prepositions *italicized*):
> **The scent** *of* the roses <u>is</u> very pleasant.
> **The promises** *of* justice *that* <u>were</u> so strongly made <u>have</u> thus far gone unfulfilled.

In harder cases (when the sentence starts with a preposition or as part of a question), the subject may come after the verb:

> *In* the yard <u>are</u> **three dogs**.
> *Where* <u>is</u> **the pack** *of* dogs?

Understanding Tenses:

Tense	Usage	Example
Present	happening now	I take the ACT.
Past	completed before now	I took the ACT.
Future	will happen	I will take the ACT.
Present Perfect	started in the past and continues now	I have taken the ACT.
Past Perfect	happened before something else in the past	I had taken the ACT when I graduated.
Conditional	could happen or have happened	If I studied, then I would have passed

Pronouns

Pronouns are words that replace nouns, like **I**, **you**, **he**, **she**, **it**, **we**, or **they**.

Rule 1: In order for a pronoun to be used correctly, there must be one clear item that it refers to in the sentence, and the pronoun must agree with that item in number. Singular items should be referred to with **it**, **its**, **or this**, while plural items should be referred to with **they**, **their**, or **these**.

> *Example*:
> **Incorrect**: The largest living primate, **the eastern lowland gorilla** has been reported to grow up to 600 pounds, but **they** are now an endangered species.
> **Correct**: The largest living primate, **the eastern lowland gorilla** has been reported to grow up to 600 pounds, but **it** is now an endangered species.

Rule 2: When deciding between **I** and **me**, just take out the other person involved. Whenever you see "between" or "among," you must use **me** instead of **I**.

> *Example*:
> **Incorrect**: Mom gave Sara and **I** presents.
> **Correct**: Mom gave Sara and **me** presents.

> **Who vs. whom**: The technical difference between 'who' and 'whom' is that 'who' is the subject pronoun, while 'whom' is the object pronoun, much like the difference between 'he' and 'him.' If this is difficult for you to grasp, don't worry: you can get ACT questions right by simply remembering that 'whom' should come directly after prepositions, in phrases like, 'to whom,' 'for whom,' 'with whom,' 'of whom,' 'by whom,' and so on. In all other cases, choose 'who.'

Possessives

Rule 1: 's means singular possessive

    Example: Tom's car is green.

Rule 2: s' means plural possessive

    Example: The students' cars are parked outside.

Three exceptions:

1. it's = it is; its = possessive form of it

    Examples: It's hot outside.
               The dog wags its tail.

2. who's = who is; whose = possessive form of who

    Examples: Who's coming to the party?
               I'm not sure whose keys these are.

3. there's = there is; their = possessive form of they

    Examples: There's an important meeting tonight.
               The musicians toured with their band.

Modifiers

A modifier is another way of referring to a description in a sentence.

Rule: When describing something in a sentence, the description should be next to the item it describes.

Example:
Incorrect: Although fascinated by the bonobos and okapis, the rare silver-back gorillas were really what drew the team of veterinarians to the remote jungle area.
Correct: Although fascinated by the bonobos and okapis, the team of

> Note: the major exception to this rule is a comma followed by an "-ing" description, which actually describes the subject of the sentence.
>
> *Example*: The tornado swept through the town, destroying trees, barns, and even houses.

Parallelism

Rule: When listing, comparing, or ordering items in a sentence, you must make sure that these different parts are parallel - or comparable - parts of speech.

Example:
Incorrect: The value of the dollar has been hurt **by the rise of the Euro** and **because there is an increase in inflation**.
Correct: The value of the dollar has been hurt **by the rise of the Euro** and **the increase in inflation**.

Redundancy

The ACT loves to test redundancy (repetition).

Rule: Whenever there is something that is repetitive in a sentence, it should be removed.

Example:
Incorrect: A new World Health Organization report claims that each year air pollution is linked to 7 million premature deaths annually.
Correct: A new World Health Organization report claims that air pollution is linked to 7 million premature deaths annually.

Adjectives and Adverbs

Adjectives describe nouns, while adverbs (usually ending in "-ly") describe verbs, nouns, adjectives or other adverbs. Learn the table of irregular adverbs below!

Adjective	Adverb
good	well
fast	fast
hard	hard
late	late
early	early
daily	daily
wrong	wrong/wrongly

Example:

Incorrect: Wanting to make a good first impression, Clark made sure to shake Alice's father's hand **firm—though not too firm**.

Correct: Wanting to make a good first impression, Clark made sure to shake Alice's father's hand **firmly—though not too firmly.**

In this sentence, we are describing how Clark shook Alice's father's hand, and 'to shake' is a verb, or action, so we must use the adverb "firmly."

Problem Set 1: Adjectives and Adverbs

One of the reasons I hate playing sports in the

middle of summer is that I have to be outside in

the <u>humidly heat</u> all day.
  1

1. A. NO CHANGE
   B. humid heat
   C. hotly humidity
   D. humid hot

The unpredictable nature of tornadoes makes

studying them a <u>continually</u> challenge.
                    2

2. F. NO CHANGE
   G. continuously
   H. continual
   J. continue

The employees of the restaurant agree that the

service has to be <u>good</u> to ensure success.
                   3

3. A. NO CHANGE
   B. positively well
   C. more good
   D. as well as we can make it

I got a new snowboard for Christmas, but I

have not used it yet because I am waiting for

<u>fresher fallen</u> snow.
  4

4. F. NO CHANGE
   G. freshly fallened
   H. newly fallen
   J. newer falling

In the New York skyline, you can see

hundreds of individual buildings, each one

shaped <u>slight different</u>.
        5

5. A. NO CHANGE
   B. slight differently.
   C. slightly more different.
   D. slightly differently.

Problem Set 1: Adjectives and Adverbs

Since the garden I keep has a wide variety of

flowers, <u>I particularly value</u> the bees' ability to

         6

pollinate plants.

6. F. NO CHANGE
   G. I value particular
   H. in particularly, I value
   J. I value, in particularly

The use of BPAs in plastics must be <u>gradual and</u>

         7

phased out to keep cancer risks at bay.

7. A. NO CHANGE
   B. gradually and
   C. gradually
   D. gradual

For his livelihood, he waited tables, but he most

enjoyed the <u>long, magnificence</u> nights he spent

         8

playing trumpet at the jazz club.

8. F. NO CHANGE
   G. long magnificence
   H. magnificently, long
   J. long, magnificent

The outpost gives conservationists an opportunity

to study the <u>magnificence</u> wolves in their natural

         9

habitat.

9. A. NO CHANGE
   B. magnificent
   C. magnificently
   D. magnificenter

<u>His affectionately</u> jokes that studying the wild

   10

wolves, which he often does for hours at a time, is

like watching a reality TV show.

10. F. NO CHANGE
    G. He affectionate
    H. His affectionate
    J. He affectionately

Problem Set 1: Adjectives and Adverbs

The New York Times is riddled with factual
                                        11

inaccurate.
    11

11. A. NO CHANGE
    B. factually inaccuracies.
    C. factual inaccuracies.
    D. factually inaccurate.

Patents emerged for new washing machine

settings intended exclusively for difficult-to-wash
                        12

attire, like silk ties and wool sweaters.

12. F. NO CHANGE
    G. most exclusively
    H. more exclusively
    J. exclusive

Clarity

Just remember not to overcomplicate things: sentences should be as direct and simple as possible. Avoid wordiness, and remember to avoid the passive voice (Instead of "The paws were licked by the dog," say, "The dog licked its paws."). Also keep in mind that subordinate and dependent clauses ('Going down the road' or 'The coffee that is on the table') cannot be sentences on their own. Remember your sentence basics: each one needs a subject and a verb. Participles are words that are formed from verbs but used as adjectives or as parts of compound verbs ("The ACT was **annoying**." or "The **annoying** ACT is difficult."). Gerunds are basically the same as participles but are used as nouns ("**Swimming** is healthy."). Generally, these questions feature sentences that sound very bizarre. Try to find the most coherent answer, which is often the most natural-sounding, concise one.

Example:

Incorrect:
The squash team appeared to have no real heart, **for the reason being that** most of the players joined only to broaden their college ambitions.

Correct:
Because most of the players had joined only to broaden their college ambitions, the squash team appeared to have no real heart.

Remember to try to keep sentences short and direct. When trying to show that one thing causes another, use a word like "since" or "because."

Example:

Incorrect:
Stanley Kubrick, frustrated by the standards and censorship policies in America, filming most of his movies in England.

Correct:
Stanley Kubrick, frustrated by the standards and censorship policies in America, filmed most of his movies in England.

This first sentence is incorrect because 'filming' cannot stand as the primary verb in the sentence. For example, you would never say, "I reading right now." Instead, you would say "I am reading right now," or "I read right now." Similarly, this sentence must say that Stanley Kubrick filmed most of his movies in England.

Problem Set 2: Clarity

I went to the grocery store - <u>owing to the</u>
₁

<u>knowledge that</u> my eggs were no good - but they
₁

had sold out of eggs just before I got there.

1. A. NO CHANGE
   B. due to the understandable fact that
   C. because
   D. so

<u>Whether or not wanting to work for Google</u>, you
₂

have to be willing to push yourself.

2. F. NO CHANGE
   G. If you want to work for Google,
   H. Wanting to work for Google, if you do,
   J. Having decided whether or not you want to work for Google,

His leg hurt <u>due to the fact that</u> it was broken.
₃

3. A. NO CHANGE
   B. because of the fact that
   C. as a result of being
   D. because

<u>Which</u> of the two essays was perfect, but at least
₄

both of the students made an attempt.

4. F. NO CHANGE
   G. Not each
   H. Neither
   J. Either

<u>Imagining all these people, it is that I know that</u>
₅

<u>they</u> have come here just to watch me play.
₅

5. A. NO CHANGE
   B. It being that I imagine all these people they
   C. Imagining all these people, they
   D. I imagine that all these people

Though we remained <u>friendly, but</u> we never spent
₆

much time together after that.

6. F. NO CHANGE
   G. friendly and
   H. friendly that
   J. friendly,

Problem Set 2: Clarity

To speak of tow-in surfing.
                        7

7. A. NO CHANGE
    B. The tow-in surfing to speak of.
    C. I'm speaking of tow-in surfing.
    D. Speaking of tow-in surfing.

The exact recipes for each delicious flavor are
                                              8

zealously guarded by ice cream manufacturers
    8

like Ben and Jerry's.

8. F. NO CHANGE
    G. To achieve each delicious flavor means that
        the exact recipes are zealously guarded
    H. The exact recipes are zealously guarded for
        how each delicious flavor
    J. Exactly how the recipes are made to have
        such delicious

Usually a pack of rescue dogs that is gathered on
                              9

the donated couches, regardless of the time of

day.

9. A. NO CHANGE
    B. dogs who
    C. dogs, and they
    D. dogs

Flash drives that are filled with final papers,
            10

music files, and pictures from my past.

10. F. NO CHANGE
    G. which have been
    H. are
    J. OMIT the underlined portion

Evidence that SUV manufacturers are playing up

the rugged image, found in the names of their
            11

vehicles: Yukon, Xterra, Pathfinder, Excursion,

and Tahoe.

11. A. NO CHANGE
    B. image is
    C. image being
    D. image, having been

Problem Set 2: Clarity

In 1965 in San Jose, California, <u>where</u> the
                                      12
Grateful Dead played their first live performance

at one of Ken Kesey's parties.

12. F. NO CHANGE
    G. was where
    H. and
    J. OMIT the underlined portion

Architect John A. <u>Roebling, who died</u> of tetanus
                              13
before his design for the Brooklyn Bridge was

completed in 1883.

13. A. NO CHANGE
    B. Roebling died
    C. Roebling dying
    D. Roebling, dead

<u>Decompression sickness,</u> an illness resulting from
                14
the formation of bubbles of inert gases within

body tissues, by itself was responsible for 14

deaths during construction of the bridge.

14. F. NO CHANGE
    G. Decompression sickness was
    H. Although decompression sickness was
    J. Decompression sickness is

Mestral was hiking with his <u>dog when he noticed</u>
                                        15
that burrs were clinging to his dog's fur and his

pants.

15. A. NO CHANGE
    B. dog and noticing
    C. dog, when noticing
    D. dog while noticing

This network of <u>spies,</u> known commonly as the
                      16
Culper Ring, provided information to General

Washington on the activities of the British forces

in New York City.

16. F. NO CHANGE
    G. spies
    H. spies was
    J. spies, had been

Problem Set 2: Clarity

In the early 1900s, <u>Brother Matthias Boutlier</u>
₁₇

<u>taught</u> baseball at the St. Mary's Industrial School
₁₇

for Boys, a young boy named George Herman

Ruth joined the team.

17. A. NO CHANGE
    B. which Brother Matthias Boutlier taught
    C. while Brother Matthias Boutlier was teaching
    D. Brother Matthias Boutlier was teaching

My friends and I were amazed by the young

basketball player <u>throwing</u> alley-oops to himself
₁₈

off the backboard.

18. Which of the following alternatives to the underlined portion would NOT be acceptable?
    F. who threw
    G. as he threw
    H. threw
    J. who was throwing

The stage <u>which has been</u> occupied by rock stars,
₁₉

country phenoms, and stand-up comedians.

19. A. NO CHANGE
    B. that is
    C. is
    D. OMIT the underlined portion

Last year, one of the guest <u>speakers being</u>
₂₀

Rodolfo Hinostroza, who came from Lima, Peru.

20. F. NO CHANGE
    G. speakers was
    H. speakers, named
    J. speakers, and

Evidence that some energy drink brands have

tried to market their products as <u>"extreme" being</u>
₂₁

found in the names of the drinks: Rockstar,

Monster, Full Throttle, and Adrenaline Rush.

21. A. NO CHANGE
    B. "extreme" is
    C. "extreme," having been
    D. "extreme,"

Problem Set 2: Clarity

Answering the fake phone call in front of the child, <u>Grandma loves</u> to pretend that she is finding
₂₂
out her grandchildren were misbehaving in school.

22. F. NO CHANGE
    G. loving
    H. having loved
    J. Grandma has loved

As we cruised together through the quiet bay that evening, thousands of microscopic <u>dinoflagellates</u>
₂₃
<u>flashing</u> brightly in the water.
₂₃

23. A. NO CHANGE
    B. dinoflagellates, which flashed
    C. dinoflagellates that flashed
    D. dinoflagellates flashed

He was searching for signs of great <u>whites when</u>
₂₄
<u>he noticed</u> a dark shadow, as long as the boat, in
₂₄
the murky water below.

24. F. NO CHANGE
    G. whites, when
    H. whites, while seeing
    J. whites when noticing

The Gobi Desert is also very famous, perhaps because it extends through two countries — China and Mongolia — <u>and containing</u> several unique
₂₅
species of wildlife.

25. A. NO CHANGE
    B. but contains
    C. and contains
    D. and

The trail <u>being overgrown with weeds and</u>
₂₆
difficult to follow.

26. F. NO CHANGE
    G. was overgrown with weeds and is
    H. is overgrown with weeds and
    J. overgrown with weeds and

Problem Set 2: Clarity

Sally turned her bike and rode back to the store

<u>being that place from which</u> she had just bought
₂₇

the necklace.

27. A. NO CHANGE
    B. from which
    C. from where
    D. it being where

<u>After a recent debacle involving</u> half of my life
₂₈

savings, my father convinced me not to invest all

of my money into one stock.

28. F. NO CHANGE
    G. Recently, a debacle that involved
    H. A recent debacle involved
    J. A recent debacle involving

The streets <u>with which the houses faced</u> would
₂₉

remain well-lit throughout the night.

29. A. NO CHANGE
    B. that the houses faced
    C. toward the houses faced
    D. with the houses facing

Over the years, I have gained notoriety <u>that</u> among
₃₀

my family and friends as a wonderful chef.

30. F. NO CHANGE
    G. which is
    H. that is
    J. OMIT the underlined portion

The Great Gatsby movie ends with Gatsby

looking out to sea as if <u>one is waiting</u> for
₃₁

someone.

31. A. NO CHANGE
    B. they were waiting
    C. the waited
    D. waiting

Problem Set 2: Clarity

<u>It is suggested that Faulkner's novels were</u> also
₃₂

gifted with the ability to capture the cadence of

human thought on paper.

32. Which choice provides the most concise and
    stylistically effective wording here?
    F. NO CHANGE
    G. It is suggested by Faulkner's novels that he
        was
    H. There is the suggestion in Faulkner's novels
        that he was
    J. Faulkner's novels suggest that he was

In fact, this area in Wyoming, one of the most

popular breeding grounds for wolves in the entire

continent, <u>that is</u> called Wolf Alley.
₃₃

33. A. NO CHANGE
    B. Delete underlined portion
    C. is
    D. which has been

Amazingly even tourists might see a dire wolf, a

grey wolf, or <u>someone watching the wolves could</u>
₃₄

<u>indeed sight</u> a wolf giving birth.
₃₄

34. F. NO CHANGE
    G. even
    H. exceptionally
    J. along with those other wolves they might
        possibly spot

<u>Start to finish, the game is taking to play about</u>
₃₅

<u>three hours.</u>
₃₅

35. A. NO CHANGE
    B. The game is played start to finish in about
        three hours.
    C. The game takes about three hours to play,
        start to finish.
    D. About three hours, is what it takes start to
        finish to play the game.

Problem Set 2: Clarity

The seemingly unique habits of the platypus

suggest <u>that belonging</u> to a different class of

      ₃₆

animals altogether.

36. F. NO CHANGE
    G. the manner in which belonging
    H. which had belonged
    J. that it belongs

The greater <u>the pressure from the wind,</u> causes

                   ₃₇

tornadoes to form faster in this situation than in all

others.

37. A. NO CHANGE
    B. pressure from the wind, which
    C. the pressure, as the wind
    D. pressure from the wind

Bundled up in wool sweaters and thick <u>coats, and</u>

                                     ₃₈

<u>we watched</u> the meteor shower from the top of our

₃₈

roof.

38. F. NO CHANGE
    G. coats while watching
    H. coats, we watched
    J. coats watching

The art collector showed the artist's sculptures

to art dealers in the United States, <u>the places in</u>

                                        ₃₉

<u>which</u> art galleries were soon offering the artist

₃₉

thousands of dollars for them.

39. A. NO CHANGE
    B. and it would happen here that
    C. where
    D. DELETE the underlined portion

It is a new style of <u>singing that performed</u> mostly

                           ₄₀

in smaller, intimate venues.

40. F. NO CHANGE
    G. singing in which it is performed
    H. singing, performing
    J. singing, performed

Problem Set 2: Clarity

Most are there to watch a game; a few are likely

to be music junkies <u>they come to</u> hear a concert in
₄₁

the stadium.

41. A. NO CHANGE
    B. there to
    C. whom
    D. they

The location of Ibiza—to the east of Spain,

between the Balearic and Mediterranean seas—

makes it a critical port city <u>and</u> vacation spot.
₄₂

42. F. NO CHANGE
    G. also for use as a
    H. additionally a
    J. and for

<u>Farmers findings that "trap crops"</u> offer an
₄₃

effective alternative to pesticides.

43. A. NO CHANGE
    B. Farmers have found that "trap crops"
    C. Farmers, having found that "trap crops"
    D. "Trap crops" are farmer's findings that

Teaching astronauts how to withstand excruciating

gravitational <u>forces, it</u> is essential to every space
₄₄

mission.

44. F. NO CHANGE
    G. forces
    H. forces that which
    J. forces, it is this which

The smallest sovereign state in the world,

<u>considering</u> Vatican City is only 1/12 the size of
₄₅

Armonk.

45. A. NO CHANGE
    B. given this characteristic
    C. and
    D. DELETE the underlined portion

Orion's belt was next, <u>with its</u> distinct alignment
₄₆

of straight stars.

46. F. NO CHANGE
    G. being its
    H. it had a
    J. whether it's a

Problem Set 2: Clarity

Business was soon booming, <u>along with</u> 10 out of
₄₇

10 tables filled at all hours of the night.

47. A. NO CHANGE
    B. so
    C. as well as
    D. with

It has been proven that <u>when walking</u> on the
₄₈

sidewalk decreases one risk of being run over.

48. F. NO CHANGE
    G. by walking
    H. walking
    J. having walked

Building a cage-free zoo, by definition, <u>meaning</u>
₄₉

<u>placing</u> humans in captivity while they view the
₄₉

animals.

49. A. NO CHANGE
    B. meant placing
    C. meaning to place
    D. meant that placing

Comparative and Superlative

When two things are being compared, the comparative form (typically ending in "-er") is used, and we always follow that with "than" (The ACT is newer than the SAT). Only when selecting one from a group of three or more can we use the superlative form (typically ending in "-est"). Remember that comparisons should be parallel, so nouns should be compared to nouns, verbs to verbs, and so on. Also remember that only one comparative or superlative can be used at once.

Example:

Incorrect:
Between the two, Speedy is easily the fastest runner; in fact, he is the faster runner in the school.

Correct:
Between the two, Speedy is easily the faster runner; in fact, he is the fastest runner in the school.

"Between the two" shows that we must use a direct comparison (the -er words). Likewise, there are many people in a school, so he would be the fastest (the -est superlative) of the whole group.

Example:

Incorrect:
The ACT is the most hardest test I have ever taken.

Correct:
The ACT is the hardest test I have ever taken.

2019-1

Problem Set 3: Comparative and Superlative

My boss never had the exact amount of lumber that he needed for a project. Instead, he always had too <u>much or too</u> few pieces.
₁

1. A. NO CHANGE
    B. many or too fewer
    C. many or too few
    D. much or few

<u>One of the scariest</u> movies of all time is Stanley
₂
Kubrick's *The Shining*.

2. F. NO CHANGE
    G. One of the most scariest
    H. The most scary
    J. The scariest

Although I had never met <u>more of the people who</u>
₃
were at the party, a few of them were close friends.

3. A. NO CHANGE
    B. more of the people whom
    C. most of the people who
    D. most of the people whom

I have been to the mall many times before, but I noticed today that the stores were <u>far more busier</u>
₄
than usual, perhaps because it is the week before Christmas.

4. F. NO CHANGE
    G. far busier
    H. more busier
    J. most busiest

Greeted by more <u>then 50,000 other</u> Indian
₅
citizens in the coastal town of Dandi, Mahatma Gandhi and his followers had finally reached the end of their momentous salt march.

5. A. NO CHANGE
    B. then 50,000 more
    C. than 50,000 more
    D. than 50,000 other

Problem Set 3: Comparative and Superlative

The cooler contained <u>too little</u> ice for the drinks to
₆

stay cold.

6. F. NO CHANGE
   G. too few
   H. lesser
   J. fewer

It's no secret that there's a <u>fairer</u> clear link
₇

between smoking and lung cancer.

7. A. NO CHANGE
   B. fair
   C. more fairly
   D. fairly

And with hundreds of hostels in your home state,

exploring is <u>easy then</u> you might imagine.
₈

8. F. NO CHANGE
   G. easier than
   H. easy than
   J. easier then

The pressure from the wind causes tornadoes to

form <u>quick</u> in this situation than in all others.
₉

9. A. NO CHANGE
   B. more quickly
   C. most quickly
   D. quickest

As we neared the finish line, the whole group of

bikers—thinly spread across the route for <u>most</u> of
₁₀

the race—condensed, forming a tight pack across

the road.

10. F. NO CHANGE
    G. the most part
    H. majority
    J. more

Problem Set 3: Comparative and Superlative

Ashley helped her family with the money she

earned babysitting, but she wanted to do <u>more so.</u>
₁₁

11. A. NO CHANGE
    B. more then that.
    C. more of them.
    D. more.

Patents emerged for washing machine settings

intended <u>exclusively</u> for difficult-to-wash attire,
₁₂

like silk ties and wool sweaters.

12. F. NO CHANGE
    G. most exclusively
    H. more exclusively
    J. exclusive

Idioms

The phrase "idiom" is short for idiomatic expression - which sounds like idiot for a reason. Idioms are phrases that we say a certain way, but there is no logical explanation why. For example, after "both" we always say "and." Therefore, it is correct to say "The ACT is both boring and silly" but incorrect to say "The ACT is both boring as well as silly." If you miss an idiom question, just try to memorize what you missed and move on - there are thousands of idioms in English, so you could spend ages trying to learn them all. Luckily, the ACT tends to test idioms that are relatively common and usually only has a few idiom questions on each test.

Example:

Incorrect:
The new Kanye West album is neither original or enjoyable.

Correct:
The new Kanye West album is neither original nor enjoyable.

In English, we always say "nor" after "neither."

2019-1

Problem Set 4: Idioms

<u>As with</u> all arguments, the best solution was clear
₁

communication between both parties.

1. A. NO CHANGE
   B. Similarly to
   C. In the same way as
   D. According with

If you'd like to go to the baseball game tomorrow

evening, you had hope that it <u>better</u> not rain.
₂

2. The best placement for the underlined portion would be:
   F. where it is now
   G. after the word *you*
   H. after the word *had*
   J. after the word *not*

When Justin Bieber was a child, his mother

<u>made a living</u> working a series of low-paying
₃

office jobs, raising her son in low-income

housing.

3. Which of the following alternatives to the underlined portion would NOT be acceptable?
   A. earned a living by
   B. made a living from
   C. made a living on
   D. earned a living

<u>In</u> the dawn of an early May morning, Yuichiro
₄

Miura became the first person to ski down Mt.

Everest, traveling 6,600 feet in just 2 minutes 20

seconds before tumbling another 1,300 feet.

4. F. NO CHANGE
   G. On
   H. With
   J. From

Echolocation, the form of communication most

often associated with dolphins, <u>by themselves</u>
₅

<u>perform</u> several key functions for the aquatic
₅

mammals.

5. A. NO CHANGE
   B. on themselves perform
   C. on itself performs
   D. by itself performs

Problem Set 4: Idioms

Duck call manufacturers have created both wood and acrylic instruments to imitate the four basic duck calls, even creating slight variations on the designs <u>in hopes of communicating</u> with the various different species of ducks.

6.   F. NO CHANGE
     G. in hopes to communicate
     H. with the hope to communicate
     J. to hope to communicate

The Getty Villa in Malibu, California is modeled <u>as</u> a first-century Roman country house, the Villa dei Papiri, which was buried by the eruption of Mt. Vesuvius.

7.   A. NO CHANGE
     B. on
     C. for
     D. with

The Board of Directors is full of plenty of different personalities, and members must be ready to <u>sprint the distance in favor of</u> their opinions.

8.   F. NO CHANGE
     G. contend in spirit
     H. be argumentative toward
     J. argue spiritedly for

Just last week, a delegate from the United States was able to sit across the conference table <u>to</u> a delegate from North Korea.

9.   A. NO CHANGE
     B. with
     C. for
     D. from

Problem Set 4: Idioms

The sun's rays are intense, capable of damaging

the skin of anyone with extensive exposure <u>to</u>
₁₀

them.

10. F. NO CHANGE
    G. on
    H. with
    J. of

The participants in the mascot race all try very

hard; it's not <u>as if</u> the mascot's efforts matter
₁₁

much, though, since the crowd never pays

attention.

11. A. NO CHANGE
    B. as
    C. as in
    D. as to

The stolen fire truck <u>resulted</u> in a ditch two towns
₁₂

over.

12. F. NO CHANGE
    G. accomplished a result of being
    H. ended up
    J. worked out

Before placement in the piano, the replacement

key must <u>be equal in length</u> to the original,
₁₃

damaged key.

13. A. NO CHANGE
    B. equal the length
    C. equal in length
    D. equal

The bioluminescent algae lit our path <u>like</u> tiny
₁₄

torches guiding us home.

14. F. NO CHANGE
    G. just as
    H. as like
    J. such as

Problem Set 4: Idioms

<u>In</u> the middle of a sunny October afternoon, Doc
15

Holliday prepared for what would come to be

known as the "Gunfight at the OK Corral."

15. A. NO CHANGE
    B. On
    C. With
    D. From

Like all Muslims, we had waited years to make

our journey <u>across</u> holy land to Mecca.
16

16. Which of the following alternatives to the
    underlined portion would NOT be acceptable?
    F. over
    G. on
    H. among
    J. through

Over one million wildebeests attempt to journey

across the crocodile-filled Mara River to Kenya,

<u>upon which</u> the animals migrate from Tanzania.
17

17. A. NO CHANGE
    B. from which
    C. when
    D. into which

The all-male city public schools are modeled <u>for</u>
18

British boarding schools.

18. F. for
    G. with
    H. by
    J. on

Just yesterday I stopped at an ice cream shop

across the street <u>with</u> the side entrance to the
19

park.

19. A. NO CHANGE
    B. from
    C. to
    D. on

Problem Set 4: Idioms

The sun produces ultraviolet radiation, which can

be harmful to anyone with extensive exposure <u>to</u>
                                                 20
it.

20. F. NO CHANGE
    G. of
    H. on
    J. with

The new computer system prompted users to

complain <u>about</u> the interface.
          21

21. A. NO CHANGE
    B. to
    C. with
    D. on

She focused her skills, imagination, and

intelligence <u>to</u> finding a way to make college more
              22
affordable for those in need.

22. F. NO CHANGE
    G. at
    H. on
    J. for

U.S. News and World Report had an orderly

scheme <u>about</u> the ranking of colleges.
        23

23. A. NO CHANGE
    B. of
    C. by
    D. for

In order to know whether to evacuate, we needed

to size <u>up to</u> the approaching hurricane.
         24

24. F. NO CHANGE
    G. up
    H. the extent of
    J. OMIT the underlined portion

Of the numerous early car inventors, Henry Ford

is credited by most history <u>textbooks, turning</u> the
                             25
tide against horse-drawn carriages.

25. A. NO CHANGE
    B. textbooks, it was he who turned
    C. textbooks with turning
    D. textbooks he turned

Problem Set 4: Idioms

His goal was to channel the surfing vibe of the

1960s California lifestyle of which he had been

<u>apart</u>.
₂₆

26. F. NO CHANGE
    G. pieces.
    H. apiece.
    J. a part.

As envisioned, the <u>store really flashed its lights</u>
₂₇

<u>on</u> young skaters, many of whom, including
₂₇

Stacy Peralta, would become the vanguard of 80's

skating culture.

27. A. NO CHANGE
    B. store paid attention with
    C. store tried to keep its focus on
    D. store's sold products were first off

In 1990, <u>in an attempt</u> to save the store, North
₂₈

moved it to a new location with a new partner,

Andrew Wexler, who wanted the store to reflect a

more grunge aesthetic.

28. Which of the following alternatives to the
    underlined portion would NOT be acceptable?
    F. attempting
    G. in attempting
    H. making an attempt
    J. for attempting

At the restaurant, we were served plates <u>piled</u>
₂₉

<u>high on</u> spaghetti and felt both overwhelmed and
₂₉

excited by the overabundance of food.

29. A. NO CHANGE
    B. piling high with
    C. piled high with
    D. piling high on

For many reasons, there's <u>increasing agreement</u>
₃₀

<u>with the view</u> that saving the environment is
₃₀

everyone's responsibility.

30. F. NO CHANGE
    G. agreement increasing with the view
    H. agreement with the view increasing
    J. agreement with the increasing view

Problem Set 4: Idioms

I simply feel better <u>to know</u> a rubber band is
₃₁
handy. Who knows when they will snap?

31. A. NO CHANGE
    B. to know that
    C. known that
    D. knowing

He is best remembered for making it possible for

hundreds of athletes <u>focused</u> on their lives and
₃₂
their sports without worrying about their medical

treatment.

32. F. NO CHANGE
    G. concentrating
    H. concentrate
    J. to concentrate

Misplaced Modifiers

"Misplaced modifiers" is a fancy way of saying that descriptions in a sentence should go right next to the object that they describe. Note that when correcting a misplaced modifier, you are allowed to use the passive voice for the only time on this test. The one major exception to putting a description next to the object it describes is that if you add an "-ing" description to the end of the sentence after a comma, then that will describe the subject of the sentence (i.e. The hurricane ripped through the small Oklahoma town, destroying most of the homes and businesses).

Example:

Incorrect:
Speeding so as to make her appointment on time, a waiting police officer pulled Sarah over.

Correct:
Speeding so as to make her appointment on time, Sarah was pulled over by a waiting police officer.

"Speeding so as to make her appointment on time" is a description of Sarah, not the waiting police officer. Therefore, Sarah's name should come right after that description.

Problem Set 5: Misplaced Modifiers

Even as a youth, Johnson loved to race

motorcycles, and as a young adult, <u>he honed his</u>
                                            1

<u>racing skills</u> on the off-road truck racing circuits.
1

1.
- A. NO CHANGE
- B. his racing skills were honed
- C. his skill in racing was honed
- D. the honing of his racing skills occurred

<u>In 1997, Hastings came up with his idea for an</u>
                    2

<u>internet-based movie rental service</u>, a time when
                 2

the rental market was still dominated by large

retail stores like Blockbuster.

2.
- F. NO CHANGE
- G. Hastings came up in 1997, with an idea for an internet-based movie rental service,
- H. The idea came to Hastings in 1997 that an internet-based movie rental service should be created,
- J. Hastings came up with the idea for an internet-based movie rental service in 1997,

Usually set off by the town or city's police force,

<u>citizens were warned of incoming attacks by an</u>
                    3

<u>air raid siren.</u>
3

3.
- A. NO CHANGE
- B. the purpose of the air raid siren was to warn citizens of incoming attacks.
- C. warning of the citizens is accomplished, in preparation for incoming attacks, by the air raid siren.
- D. the air raid sirens warned citizens of incoming attacks.

After removing the old, damaged CPU heat sink,

<u>thermal paste–just a touch–is applied.</u>
              4

4.
- F. NO CHANGE
- G. the technician applies a touch of thermal paste.
- H. the application of a touch of thermal paste is next.
- J. a touch of thermal paste is applied by the technician.

The walls were lined with <u>other climbers'</u>
                              5

<u>images</u> — many of them the heroes who had
5

inspired me to pursue such an arduous trek.

5.
- A. NO CHANGE
- B. images of other climbers
- C. other climbers whose images were captured
- D. images in which other climbers were present

Problem Set 5: Misplaced Modifiers

As we neared the finish line, <u>the crowd cheered</u>
6

<u>as, held together with glue and nails, our cart</u>
6

<u>sped into the lead.</u>
6

6. F. NO CHANGE
   G. as the crowd cheered, our cart sped into the lead held together with nails and glue.
   H. as the crowd cheered, held together with glue and nails, our cart sped to the lead.
   J. our cart, held together with glue and nails, sped into the lead as the crowd cheered.

Laughing under my breath at my coach's

sarcastic comment, <u>the race picked up speed</u> and
7

soon crossed the finish line.

7. A. NO CHANGE
   B. the speed picked up
   C. I picked up speed
   D. the race finally was picking up speed

At age three, Wolfgang Amadeus Mozart would

sit in fascination and watch his older sister's

piano lessons with their father, Leopold. Noticing

this interest, <u>Wolfgang began working with</u>
8

<u>Leopold to learn a few minuets.</u>
8

8. F. NO CHANGE
   G. Leopold began teaching Wolfgang a few minuets.
   H. a few minuets were taught to Wolfgang by Leopold.
   J. he began teaching him a few minuets.

Having recently moved to Alaska, <u>and finding</u>
9

myself living in an Arctic environment for the

first time.

9. A. NO CHANGE
   B. I find
   C. having found
   D. finding

After observing Voodoo practices in the

Caribbean, <u>Zora Neale Hurston included many of</u>
10

<u>these traditions in her own novels.</u>
10

10. F. NO CHANGE
    G. many of these traditions were included in Zora Neale Hurston's novels.
    H. the novels of Zora Neale Hurston included many of these traditions.
    J. they were included in Zora Neale Hurston's novels.

Problem Set 5: Misplaced Modifiers

Lord of the Flies is meant to evoke both the

primitivism inherent in man <u>stranded together on</u>
₁₁

<u>an island</u> and the book of the same name, which
₁₁

tells the story of a group of young boys.

11. The best placement for the underlined portion
    would be:
    A. where it is now.
    B. after the word *book*.
    C. after the word story.
    D. after the word *boys* (ending the sentence
       with a period).

Just last week I stood in line behind a man who

was drawing beautiful sketches in a <u>bright yellow</u>
₁₂

<u>hat in a</u> notebook.
₁₂

12. The best placement for the underlined portion
    would be:
    F. where it is now.
    G. after the word *man*.
    H. after the word *was*.
    J. after the word *notebook* (ending the
       sentence with a period).

If you <u>recently visit Madison Square Garden, as I</u>
₁₃

<u>did,</u> you will see the two new sky bridges
₁₃

suspended from the ceiling.

13. A. NO CHANGE
    B. visit Madison Square Garden, recently, as I
       did,
    C. visit Madison Square Garden, as I did
       recently,
    D. visit recently, as I did, Madison Square
       Garden,

Weighing almost one million pounds and orbiting

Earth at over 17,000 miles per hour, <u>scientists</u>
₁₄

<u>in the International Space Station are offered</u> a
₁₄

unique opportunity to conduct experiments in

biology, physics, chemistry and meteorology.

14. F. NO CHANGE
    G. the International Space Station offers
       scientists
    H. scientists researching at the International
       Space Station are offered
    J. research scientists at the International Space
       Station are offered

Problem Set 5: Misplaced Modifiers

<u>Some</u> time later, Rebecca finally admitted she ate
₁₅

the last cookie.

15. A. NO CHANGE
    B. Since some
    C. After some
    D. For some

<u>Speed was already understood to be a key to big</u>
₁₆

<u>wave surfing by Laird Hamilton.</u>
₁₆

16. F. NO CHANGE
    G. As Laird Hamilton already understood, that speed is a key to big wave surfing.
    H. Laird Hamilton already understood that speed is a key to big wave surfing.
    J. A key to big wave surfing, Laird Hamilton

By studying platypus behavior, <u>a discovery has</u>
₁₇

<u>revealed to scientists William King Gregory and</u>
₁₇

<u>David Fleay the cause of this apparent variation.</u>
₁₇

17. A. NO CHANGE
    B. the discovery of the cause of this apparent variation has been made by scientists William King Gregory and David Fleay
    C. scientists William King Gregory and David Fleay have discovered the cause of this apparent variation.
    D. the cause of this apparent variation has been discovered by scientists William King Gregory and David Fleay.

Chester made a delicious Thanksgiving feast

for 30 despite the fact that his mother joked that

he "could burn water." <u>In spite of his limited</u>
₁₈

<u>experience,</u> the holiday meal was one of the best
₁₈

that anyone in his family could remember.

18. F. NO CHANGE
    G. An impressive culinary feat,
    H. Regardless of his minimal expertise,
    J. Better known for his math skills,

Problem Set 5: Misplaced Modifiers

<u>Finally, approaching</u> Madrid, the city's medieval
₁₉

architecture came into view.

19. A. NO CHANGE
    B. Finally, as I approached
    C. Finally, to approach
    D. Approaching

<u>Introduced by me to my favorite food, with lots</u>
₂₀

<u>of sauce, I started being taught by Laura how to</u>
₂₀

<u>cook.</u>
₂₀

20. F. NO CHANGE
    G. Introducing Laura to my favorite food, with lots of sauce, she started teaching me how to cook.
    H. Teaching me how to cook, Laura was introduced by me to my favorite food, with lots of sauce.
    J. I introduced Laura to my favorite food, with lots of sauce, and she started teaching me how to cook.

<u>For him, Danny says what he wants his computer</u>
₂₁

<u>network doing, even when he sleeps, is to know a</u>
₂₁

<u>source of both pleasure and power.</u>
₂₁

21. A. NO CHANGE
    B. Even when he sleeps, Danny says that to know his computer network is doing what he wants is a source of both pleasure and power for him.
    C. Even when he sleeps, doing what he wants, is knowing his computer network is a source of both pleasure and power for Danny.
    D. Danny says that to know his computer network is doing what he wants, even when he sleeps, is a source of both pleasure and power.

<u>The New York State Assembly honored</u>
₂₂

<u>Coleman's Pub in 1878 by designating it the</u>
₂₂

<u>Borough Restaurant of Brooklyn.</u>
₂₂

22. F. NO CHANGE
    G. By designating it the Borough Restaurant of Brooklyn, 1878 was the year the New York State Assembly honored Coleman's pub.
    H. Honoring Coleman's Pub, the Borough Restaurant of Brooklyn was what it was designated by the State Assembly of New York.
    J. Designating it the Borough Restaurant of Brooklyn, Coleman's Pub was honored by the New York State Assembly in 1878.

Problem Set 5: Misplaced Modifiers

This feature extends the time that astronauts can

work <u>greatly</u> at the Space Station.
    23

23. The best placement for the underlined portion would be:
   A. where it is now
   B. after the word *feature*
   C. after the word *time*
   D. after the word *astronauts*

Noun/Pronoun Agreement

Pronouns (**I, me, you, we, it, they,** etc.) are words that replace nouns in English. Whenever we use a pronoun in a sentence, there must be one clear item to which the pronoun refers, and the pronoun should be plural or singular to match that item. Similarly, when we use nouns to describe other nouns in a sentence, they must agree in number. Take a look at the examples below to get a better idea of what we mean.

Examples

Incorrect:
The board of directors oversees the company's financial planning, and they have taken few risks in the past ten years.

Correct:
The board of directors oversees the company's financial planning, and it has taken few risks in the past ten years.

The "board of directors" is really just one board, so instead of using "they," we must use "it."

Incorrect:
The teacher gave Juan and I extra credit for our project on planetary orbits.

Correct:
The teacher gave Juan and me extra credit for our project on planetary orbits.

The trick for telling between "I" and "me," "she" and "her," or "he" and "him" is to take out the other person or people in the sentence. Would you say "the teacher gave I extra credit," or "the teacher gave me extra credit?"

Incorrect:
The Phillips twins, John and Eric, decided they wanted to be a doctor when they get older.

Correct:
The Phillips twins, John and Eric, decided they wanted to be doctors when they get older.

The Phillips twins are two people, so they couldn't decide to be one doctor. Therefore, we must say "The Phillips twins decided they wanted to be doctors."

Problem Set 6: Noun/Pronoun Agreement

Every day the hostel hosts a new group of international <u>travelers, those foreigners</u> come to explore the city.
₁

1. A. NO CHANGE
    B. travelers, who
    C. travelers, whom
    D. DELETE the underlined portion

My favorite player was always Frank Thomas, <u>who</u> played for the Chicago White Sox.
₂

2. F. NO CHANGE
    G. whom
    H. which
    J. and

Inventor Daisuke Inoue admits that while his karaoke machines can't perfectly simulate live musical performances, <u>it does</u> come close.
₃

3. A. NO CHANGE
    B. they do
    C. it has
    D. and they

As you keep practicing your forehand and backhand, you will get more comfortable with each of the strokes. <u>He or she will learn</u> how to
₄
use topspin and backspin to control the ball.

4. F. NO CHANGE
    G. We will learn
    H. You will learn
    J. People will learn

Chu loves the GPS function of his phone because it gives him directions whenever he needs. He also loves the voice dialing feature, which allows him to call <u>them</u> just by saying their names.
₅

5. A. NO CHANGE
    B. friends
    C. it
    D. their phones

Problem Set 6: Noun/Pronoun Agreement

I was friends with <u>most of the people who</u> were
₆
in my class.

6. F. NO CHANGE
   G. most of the people whom
   H. more of the people who
   J. more of the people whom

While I was growing up, my father and my

grandfather each took great pride in his own car,

constantly cleaning it or tinkering with its parts.

<u>That car</u> helped me learn everything I know about

automobiles.
₇

7. A. NO CHANGE
   B. His car
   C. Those cars
   D. This car

This bowling alley resembles an ordinary one

about as much as a wolf resembles a chihuahua.

At four stories high and a full city block across,

<u>they were</u> much larger than the alleys I have been
₈
in before.

8. F. NO CHANGE
   G. it was
   H. they are
   J. it is

The Archi language is one of the most unique in

the world, with a morphology and phonemes that

<u>makes them</u> baffling to anyone from outside the
₉
village of Archib, Russia.

9. A. NO CHANGE
   B. makes it
   C. make them
   D. make it

Problem Set 6: Noun/Pronoun Agreement

Morrison seems to identify with earlier authors

like Virginia Woolf and William Faulkner -

authors <u>which they</u> use shifting perspectives and
        10

fragmented narratives.

10. F. NO CHANGE
    G. who
    H. whom
    J. that

Andy is six, living in those two or three years

when <u>they</u> can manage to read or write but when
    11

what they're really interested in are toys and

friends.

11. A. NO CHANGE
    B. he
    C. some of them
    D. children

The human appendix is considered a vestigial

organ, so the removal of an appendix when <u>it is</u>
                    12

inflamed is not harmful to the patient.

12. F. NO CHANGE
    G. that is
    H. they are
    J. those are

Mike Kryzewski's influence as the head

basketball coach at Duke University grew, and

the program flourished <u>under its</u> guidance.
                  13

13. A. NO CHANGE
    B. under his
    C. among its
    D. among his

Then, seconds later, a new mole would pop up,

looking like <u>they were</u> taunting the frazzled
        14

player.

14. F. NO CHANGE
    G. they had been
    H. it is
    J. it was

Problem Set 6: Noun/Pronoun Agreement

"Carpetbagger" was the term used to describe

men like General Littlefield who, emboldened by

the events of the Civil War, moved south and

gained political power despite the accusations of

corruption leveled <u>against them.</u>
     15

15. A. NO CHANGE
    B. against him
    C. against you
    D. against me

Coaches provide expert voice instruction, and

students are rewarded for improving <u>his or her</u>
                                        16

tone and range.

16. F. NO CHANGE
    G. there
    H. their
    J. one's

My caffeine addiction, like most addictions, is not

without <u>it's</u> negative consequences.
         17

17. A. NO CHANGE
    B. there
    C. their
    D. its

Gabriel Voisin invented a better braking system

for aircraft in 1929. Before <u>his</u> invention, pilots
                               18

needed much longer runways to take off and land.

18. F. NO CHANGE
    G. their
    H. its'
    J. it's

Today, the restaurant acknowledges <u>its</u> Irish
                                      19

heritage by hosting cultural events and dance

competitions.

19. A. NO CHANGE
    B. its'
    C. it's
    D. their

Problem Set 6: Noun/Pronoun Agreement

During that storied age of boxing, crowds of

listeners gathered around the radio to listen to <u>its'</u>
                                                    20

favorite fighters compete.

20. F. NO CHANGE
    G. its
    H. their
    J. his or her

Each artist brought something unique to <u>their</u>
                                          21

creations.

21. A. NO CHANGE
    B. his or herselves
    C. hers or his
    D. his or her

The washing machine wasn't patented until 1908.

Before <u>their</u> invention, Americans washed all of
        22

their clothing by hand.

22. F. NO CHANGE
    G. its
    H. its'
    J. it's

Furthermore, the law firm offered no evidence

to back up <u>it's</u> assertion that there was no
            23

wrongdoing.

23. A. NO CHANGE
    B. its
    C. their
    D. they're

My instructor sat in the passenger seat as I

changed lanes on the highway for the first time. I

wasn't <u>an expert driver,</u> but at least I was an easy
         24

one to teach.

24. F. NO CHANGE
    G. a driver who drove with great skill or
       technique
    H. a master of the art of lane-changing,
    J. an expert,

Organization

Be sure to arrange ideas in a logical, fluid order. No sentence should be out of place in relation to what comes before or after it. First, look to arrange events in chronological order. Then, look for key placement words like "this," "these," "those," or "that." If you see a phrase like "this book was interesting," the phrase must directly follow something that introduces what "this book" is referencing.

Example:

Incorrect:
I started piano lessons around four years old. When I was seven, I learned violin. More instruments followed throughout my teenage years, so by the time I was twenty, I could essentially play any part in a Mozart concerto. At ten, I mastered guitar.

Correct:
I started piano lessons around four years old. When I was seven, I learned violin. At ten, I mastered guitar. More instruments followed throughout my teenage years, so by the time I was twenty, I could essentially play any part in a Mozart concerto.

Age 10 comes between age seven and this person's teenage years, so the sentence about age 10 should be between those sentences.

Problem Set 7: Organization

[1] Down the street from my high school, the Clucky Chicken is always open, and a friendly employee is always waiting. [2] It is on a quiet street, located between a large field and a gas station. [3] The field isn't intended for sports or leisure; it was once part of a large, private resort. [4] But these days, no one works at the old resort to enforce the warnings, and the townspeople all enjoy the open space. [5] Old signs are still posted around the outside threatening punishment for potential trespassers.

1. For the sake of the logic and coherence of this paragraph, Sentence 5 should be placed:
   A. where it is now
   B. before Sentence 1
   C. after Sentence 2
   D. after Sentence 3

[1] I can understand why some people might like American football more than soccer. [2] American football features many violent collisions and exciting plays. [3] However, there are also many timeouts and commercial breaks. [4] Soccer, on the other hand, has less violence but features constant movement and action. [5] Though the sport is less popular in America, it is actually the most watched in most of the world.

2. For the sake of the logic and coherence of this paragraph, Sentence 4 should be placed:
   F. where it is now
   G. after Sentence 1
   H. after Sentence 2
   J. after Sentence 5

Problem Set 7: Organization

[1] As for the alarm on her iPhone, Grandma not only uses it to wake up but also to play jokes on her grandchildren. [2] Answering the fake phone call in front of the child, Grandma loves to pretend that she is finding out her grandchildren were misbehaving at school. [3] I suppose Grandma hasn't learned all the functions of her phone, but I know she will keep trying new ones.

[1] The first country musician to gain nationwide acclaim was Vernon Dalhart. [2] He was born in Jefferson, Texas, but his family soon moved to Dallas. [3] While there, Dalhart learned to play the jaw harp and harmonica and took lessons in vocal training. [4] Dalhart married his wife Sadie in 1901, and the couple moved to New York a few years later. [5] After seeing an ad in a newspaper, Dalhart auditioned for Thomas Alva Edison and earned a contract from Edison Records. [6] Dalhart's recording of "The Wreck of the Old 97," a classic railroad ballad, became the first Southern song to be a national success.

3. Upon reviewing the paragraph and realizing that some information has been left out, the writer composes the following sentence:

> She sets the alarm to go off at a time when a grandchild will be visiting, using the same sound as her ringtone.

The most logical place for this sentence would be:
A. before Sentence 1
B. after Sentence 1
C. after Sentence 2
D. after Sentence 3

4. Upon reviewing the paragraph and realizing that some information has been left out, the writer composes the following sentence:

> Despite the great success of his early recordings, Dalhart became virtually unknown following the Great Depression.

The most logical place for this sentence would be after Sentence:
F. 2
G. 4
H. 5
J. 6

Problem Set 7: Organization

[1] Our daughter has started playing organized soccer. [2] I think only the coaches actually think of the game as "organized." [3] Sophia is six, the age when children can manage to focus on the game only if the ball is right in front of them. [4] Children at that age don't understand the concept of positions, so they just chase the ball around the field until something better, like a butterfly or an ice cream truck, grabs their attention. [5] It's not as if anyone's position matters much, though - the ball never seems to get anywhere near the goals.

5. The author wishes to add the following sentence in order to emphasize the doubt already shown about a certain idea in the paragraph:

   The rest of us know better.

   The new sentence would best be placed after Sentence:
   A. 1
   B. 2
   C. 3
   D. 5

[1] As I watched the scene in the bay, I tried sketching several of the sights: the steaming cruise ships, bustling workers, and intrigued tourists. [2] Once our vessel departed from port, I sketched the landscape of the shore. [3] None of these artistic attempts were very good, but at least I could start to make out the forms I was drawing. [4] These sketches would never make me famous, though.

6. For the sake of the logic and coherence of the paragraph, sentence 2 should be placed:
   F. where it is now
   G. before sentence 1
   H. after sentence 3
   J. after sentence 4

Problem Set 7: Organization

[1] I set mouse traps in every room, closet, and even the attic, thinking I had done enough to get rid of the rodents. [2] Every night, when I caught another one or two, I thought they would be the last. [3] Then, the next evening, I would see another one scurry across the floor.

7. Which of the following sequences of sentences makes this paragraph most logical?
   A. NO CHANGE
   B. 2, 1, 3
   C. 2, 3, 1
   D. 3, 1, 2

[1] Though the book did not have the immediate impact that Helen Hunt Jackson had hoped, A Century of Dishonor is now considered an important piece of American literature. [2] The book tells the story of seven different Native American tribes, like the Sioux and Cherokee, that were treated unfairly by white settlers. [3] Jackson decided to write the book upon hearing the story of Standing Bear, a leader of the Ponca tribe. [4] Her research led her to discover grave injustices, like the slaughter of the Praying Town Indians, who had even converted to Christianity.

8. Which of the following sequences of sentences makes this paragraph most logical?
   F. NO CHANGE
   G. 2, 1, 3, 4
   H. 2, 3, 4, 1
   J. 4, 1, 2, 3

Problem Set 7: Organization

[1] Though some devices use other means of sensing touch, most touch-screen phones use what is called a capacitive system. [2] A typical phone has a glass screen that is covered by a layer that stores electrical charge. [3] The iPhone, for instance, utilizes a grid-like capacitive layer to sense multiple touches at once. [4] Once the charge is altered, the computer uses the difference in charge at each corner to calculate the exact location of the touch. [5] When a user touches the monitor, some of the charge is transferred to the user, so the charge on the capacitive layer decreases. [6] This information is relayed to the touch-screen driver software, which interacts with the programs that are open to make the phone work.

9. For the sake of the logic and coherence of this paragraph, Sentence 4 should be placed:
    A. where it is now.
    B. after sentence 2.
    C. after sentence 5.
    D. after sentence 6.

Problem Set 7: Organization

[1] Recently, my family has joined a new angler's group active here around Lake Michigan that is dedicated to making sure recreational anglers use responsible practices when they go fishing. [2] Instead of driving with our motorboat to a nearby fishing-ground, we rent a boat when we get to our chosen spot. [3] On shore, we buy only live bait lures that are native to the lake. [4] Even with these extra precautions, fishing with my family still feels casual and relaxed. [5] We then climb into the boat and set sail.

10. For the sake of the logic and coherence of this paragraph, Sentence 5 should be placed:
   F. where it is now.
   G. after sentence 1.
   H. after sentence 2.
   J. after sentence 3.

Parallelism

When writing a sequence, comparison, or list in a sentence, all the elements of the sequence, comparison, or list must share the samestructure. Similarly, two parts of an idiomatic expression should also be parallel. Take a look at the examples below to get a better understanding.

Examples

Incorrect:
My homework for tonight includes drawing up an outline for my history paper, reading more of The Great Gatsby, and math.

Correct:
My homework for tonight includes drawing up an outline for my history paper, reading more of The Great Gatsby, and working on a few math problems.

This is incorrect because 'math' is not parallel in structure with 'drawing up an outline,' or 'reading more of The Great Gatsby.' 'Working on a few math problems,' however, makes the entire list parallel.

2019-1

Problem Set 8: Parallelism

In the 1980s, Bowie performed alternately as a

solo artist and <u>he was</u> part of a band, The Tin
    ₁

Machine.

1. A. NO CHANGE
   B. as well
   C. as
   D. being

For decades, the city had owned no stadium in

which basketball games could be played and <u>rock</u>
    ₂

<u>concerts performed.</u>
  ₂

2. F. NO CHANGE
   G. the performing of rock concerts.
   H. rock concerts were performed there.
   J. there were rock concerts performed there.

Once awake, members of the litter start to mew at

each other while looking for food, <u>they play</u> with
    ₃

their siblings, or exploring new territory.

3. A. NO CHANGE
   B. playing
   C. played
   D. play

Stalin attempted to brutally silence his critics <u>by</u>
    ₄

<u>imprisoning</u> and executing them.
  ₄

4. F. NO CHANGE
   G. through imprisonment
   H. with imprisonment
   J. in prison

The band has flown all over the world, broken

records for album sales, and <u>throwing</u> out the first
    ₅

pitch at the World Series.

5. A. NO CHANGE
   B. throw
   C. threw
   D. even thrown

Problem Set 8: Parallelism

As a vocal leader of the movement, Malcolm X encouraged his followers to challenge the established social order and <u>for learning Islam.</u>
₆

6. F. NO CHANGE
    G. Islam can be learned.
    H. to learn about Islam.
    J. for Islam to be learned.

John Smith joined the Jamestown expedition to seek profit and <u>if he would</u> continue his travels.
₇

7. A. NO CHANGE
    B. that he should
    C. was forced to
    D. to

It's impossible to predict which people will embrace the music or <u>if they were to start to</u>
₈
<u>dance,</u> and I've stopped trying to guess.
₈

8. F. NO CHANGE
    G. would have started to dance
    H. start to dance
    J. might be starting to dance

Traditional Buddhist texts and legends chronicle life, death, and <u>to have a rebirth.</u>
₉

9. A. NO CHANGE
    B. rebirth.
    C. to be reborn.
    D. to have rebirth.

Little is known about my great-grandfather except that he worked as a dairy farmer and later <u>as a</u>
₁₀
<u>magician's assisting.</u>
₁₀

10. F. NO CHANGE
    G. working as a magician's assistant.
    H. as an assistant to a magician.
    J. to assist a magician.

Problem Set 8: Parallelism

In the last decade of his career, Schulman wrote

a screenplay, East Tremont and Hopeless, which

describes how he got his start as a fighter,

<u>expresses</u> his views on the importance of family,
   11

and gives advice to aspiring fighters.

11. A. NO CHANGE
    B. he expresses
    C. express
    D. to express

From her, Josh learned <u>which college classes were</u>
                                                    12

<u>interesting and the ones that weren't to avoid.</u>
                          12

12. F. NO CHANGE
    G. which college classes were interesting and
       which were to be avoided.
    H. which college classes were interesting and
       avoiding the ones that weren't.
    J. the interesting college classes and the ones
       that weren't should be avoided.

Armstrong and Aldrin became the first astronauts

to collect moon rocks and <u>bringing</u> them back to
                                13

Earth to study.

13. A. NO CHANGE
    B. will bring
    C. bring
    D. is bringing

By the 1760s Mary Ludwig Hays was leading

nightly literacy lectures and <u>had taught</u> over three
                                    14

hundred women how to read and write.

14. F. NO CHANGE
    G. a dedication to teaching
    H. a teacher of
    J. has taught

Possessives

With singular nouns, simply add an apostrophe "s" to show ownership. For regular plural nouns (those that end in 's'), simply add an apostrophe after the "s" at the end; for special plural nouns (those that do not end in 's'), follow the rule for singular possessives. Make sure you know the information in the table that shows exceptions to these rules caused by contractions (two words combined by an apostrophe).

Examples

Incorrect:
I wanted to buy a book for my nieces birthday, so I headed for the childrens' bookstore.

Correct:
I wanted to buy a book for my niece's birthday, so I headed for the children's bookstore.

This first sentence incorrect because the birthday belongs to the niece, and 'children' is already plural.

Root word	Possessive	Contraction
it	its	it's (it is)
they	their	they're (they are)
who	whose	who's (who is)

Problem Set 9: Possessives

Our school started a fund to help Anton and his family. During the wildfires, the first story of <u>his parents</u> house had burned, leaving thousands of dollars in damage.
₁

1. A. NO CHANGE
   B. his parents'
   C. Anton's parents
   D. Antons parents

You have to admire the cleverness of a candidate <u>who's</u> campaign slogan was simply "I like Ike."
₂

2. F. NO CHANGE
   G. whose
   H. which
   J. that's

Also known as Baltimore club or "Bmore house" because of <u>its'</u> origins in the city of Baltimore,
₃
this genre combines elements of hip-hop and house music.

3. A. NO CHANGE
   B. it's
   C. it's having
   D. its

In an early morning meeting on June 5, 1944, Eisenhower ordered the troops to proceed with the following <u>days</u> invasion.
₄

4. F. NO CHANGE
   G. days'
   H. day's
   J. days's

Commercial vessels, like the Thomas Jefferson ferry, were able to reach the plane just four minutes after it touched down in the water in <u>they're attempt to rescue it's</u> passengers.
₅

5. A. NO CHANGE
   B. they're attempt to rescue its
   C. their attempt to rescue it's
   D. their attempt to rescue its

Problem Set 9: Possessives

Within <u>they're composition there's</u> plenty of
₆

room for improvisation, and members of the

quintet must be thoroughly prepared to change

tempo on the fly.

6. F. NO CHANGE
   G. that composition theirs
   H. their composition their is
   J. that composition there's

We plan the order of the <u>day's tasks</u>, one by one.
₇

7. A. NO CHANGE
   B. days tasks
   C. days tasks,
   D. task's for the day,

<u>Infants</u> first attempts at crawling always captivate
₈

the parents, who frequently assist the children in

their efforts.

8. F. NO CHANGE
   G. Infant's
   H. Infantses
   J. Infants'

The <u>dog's faces</u> were alight with hope at the
₉

prospect of food.

9. A. NO CHANGE
   B. dogs' faces
   C. dogs faces
   D. dogs face's

A little girl <u>whose</u> holding a balloon smiles as an
₁₀

ice cream truck pulls up at the corner.

10. F. NO CHANGE
    G. G. who's
    H. H. thats
    J. J. while

<u>Its</u> impossible to tickle yourself, but children will
₁₁

never stop trying.

11. A. NO CHANGE
    B. It's
    C. Its'
    D. That's

Problem Set 9: Possessives

It's extremely unlikely the snake would bite, but
₁₂

if it did, there would be no venom to really harm

the victim.

12. F. NO CHANGE
    G. It's extremely unlikely,
    H. Its extremely unlikely,
    J. Its extremely unlikely

The parents in the bleachers make a wild roar

every time the ball escapes the crowd of young

players. The children must be puzzled by the

grown-up's strange, frantic behavior.
₁₃

13. A. NO CHANGE
    B. grown-up's,
    C. grown-ups
    D. grown-ups'

I am currently working on a new musical. What
₁₄

it's about the labor movement in America in the
₁₄

late nineteenth century.

14. F. NO CHANGE
    G. Thats
    H. Its
    J. It's

Eventually, the stump of the old, dead tree will be

removed, allowing healthy grass to grow in it's
₁₅

place.

15. A. NO CHANGE
    B. grow in its
    C. have grow in its
    D. have grown in it's

The rambunctious kittens also led me to ask
₁₆

another question: what is life without time to

play?

16. F. NO CHANGE
    G. kitten's also
    H. kittens also,
    J. kittens' also

Problem Set 9: Possessives

When he was just five years old, Mozart would spend hours playing on the <u>families piano.</u>
₁₇

17. A. NO CHANGE
    B. familys piano
    C. family's piano
    D. families' piano

Towering palms, <u>who's</u> large leaves I previously
₁₈
associated with tropical paradises, grow all over the campus.

18. F. NO CHANGE
    G. whose
    H. of who's
    J. of whose

I recently adopted two kittens from the local animal shelter. Since the house I rent seems to attract mice, I particularly appreciate the <u>kittens</u>
₁₉
<u>ability</u> to hunt these pesky rodents.
₁₉

19. A. NO CHANGE
    B. kittens ability,
    C. kittens' ability
    D. kitten's ability

There is a wide array of flavors <u>to choose from</u>
₂₀
<u>with todays</u> jellybeans, including cotton candy,
₂₀
kiwi, and chocolate pudding.

20. F. NO CHANGE
    G. to choose from with todays'
    H. to choose from, with today's
    J. to choose from with today's

She learned that her <u>countrys</u> electoral system was
₂₁
very confusing.

21. A. NO CHANGE
    B. countrys'
    C. country's
    D. countries

Problem Set 9: Possessives

I often find myself in this situation—sheepishly

stroking someone <u>else's</u> hair.
     ₂₂

22. F. NO CHANGE
       G. elses'
       H. elses
       J. else

In 1993, virtual learning became a reality when

Jones International University launched <u>it's</u> first
                                ₂₃

online degree program.

23. A. NO CHANGE
       B. there
       C. its
       D. its'

My caffeine addiction, like most addictions, is not

without <u>it's</u> negative consequences.
     ₂₄

24. F. NO CHANGE
       G. there
       H. their
       J. its

Gabriel Voisin invented a better braking system

for aircraft in 1929. Before <u>his</u> invention, pilots
                           ₂₅

needed much longer runways to take off and land.

25. A. NO CHANGE
       B. their
       C. its'
       D. it's

Jeans constructed according to <u>Levi Strauss</u>
                                        ₂₆

<u>original instructions</u> are so comfortable and
   ₂₆

durable that the design of his pants has been

barely altered over time.

26. F. NO CHANGE
       G. Levi Strauss' original instructions
       H. Levi Strauss' original instructions,
       J. Levi Strauss original instructions,

Problem Set 9: Possessives

The <u>bench's</u> legs are longer on one side, so it
₂₇

wobbles when you sit on it.

27. A. NO CHANGE
    B. benches'
    C. benches
    D. bench,

I followed <u>Ms. Stern's initial instructions</u> and
₂₈

wrote my name on the test, only to realize I

couldn't even answer the first question.

28. F. NO CHANGE
    G. Ms. Sterns' initial instructions
    H. Ms. Sterns initial instructions
    J. Ms. Sterns' initial instructions,

It takes three to five days for housefly larvae to

begin <u>it's</u> pupa stage.
₂₉

29. A. NO CHANGE
    B. there
    C. they're
    D. their

Furthermore, the law firm offered no evidence

to back up <u>it's</u> assertion that there was no
₃₀

wrongdoing.

30. F. NO CHANGE
    G. its
    H. their
    J. they're

By the end of the first year, <u>Coleman's friends</u> had
₃₁

already doubled their money and were eager to

invest in a new location.

31. A. NO CHANGE
    B. Colemans friends
    C. Colemans friend's
    D. Coleman's friend's

Today, the restaurant acknowledges <u>its</u> Irish
₃₂

heritage by hosting cultural events and dance

competitions.

32. F. NO CHANGE
    G. its'
    H. it's
    J. their

Problem Set 9: Possessives

Called a "superconductor" because <u>their highly</u> ₃₃

<u>conductive</u> at low temperatures, silver is the most
₃₃

electrically conductive element in the universe.

33. A. NO CHANGE
    B. its high conductivity
    C. it's highly conductive
    D. its highly conductive

After all, these rooms are only a small portion of

the collection of biological exhibits and an even

smaller <u>portion, of the museum's</u> total collection.
₃₄

34. F. NO CHANGE
    G. portion of the museums
    H. portion of the museum's
    J. portion of the museums,

With only our headlamps to light the way, we

began to make out the shapes of the <u>stalactites' in</u>
₃₅

<u>the cave's</u> interior.
₃₅

35. A. NO CHANGE
    B. stalactite's in the caves'
    C. stalactites in the cave's
    D. stalactites in the caves

Though Alicia Keys <u>had sang about the city's</u> "big
₃₆

lights," nothing could have prepared me for Times

Square.

36. F. NO CHANGE
    G. has sang about the city's
    H. had sung about the cities
    J. sang about the city's

On Broadway, wedged between buildings many

times <u>it's</u> height, stands the Dyckman Farmhouse
₃₇

Museum.

37. A. NO CHANGE
    B. they're
    C. its
    D. their

Problem Set 9: Possessives

Ronald Reagan, however, became one of the

<u>world's most powerful and most controversial</u>
38

<u>leader's.</u>
38

38. F. NO CHANGE
G. world's most powerful and most
   controversial leaders'.
H. world's most powerful and most
   controversial leaders.
J. worlds most powerful and most
   controversial leaders.

Plato's mentor was the <u>countries most prominent</u>
39

philosopher, Socrates.

39. A. NO CHANGE
B. country's most prominent
C. countries' more prominent
D. country's most prominently

The washing machine wasn't patented until 1908.

Before <u>their</u> invention, Americans washed all of
40

their clothing by hand.

40. F. NO CHANGE
G. its
H. its'
J. it's

Popular for its efficiency and convenience, <u>Fords'</u>
41

invention pushed the modern automobile into

the American mainstream while simultaneously

obscuring the rich history of horse-drawn

carriages.

41. A. NO CHANGE
B. Ford's
C. Fords's
D. Fords

Punctuation

Remember the basics: periods end clauses, commas break up clauses or lists of three or more things, semicolons act as periods, and colons set up an example, explanation or list where the sentence could otherwise end.

Examples

Incorrect:
During the interview, I casually mentioned what a big fan I was of the company, this seemed to impress my interviewer.

Correct:

During the interview, I casually mentioned what a big fan I was of the company; this seemed to impress my interviewer.

During the interview, I casually mentioned what a big fan I was of the company, and this seemed to impress my interviewer.

During the interview, my casual mention of what a big fan I was of the company seemingly impressed my interviewer.

Problem Set 10: Punctuation

The two former gridiron heroes, who had long ago <u>retired from football, to pursue new ambitions,</u> were now starring on the national political stage.

1. A. NO CHANGE
   B. retired from football to pursue new ambitions
   C. retired from football to pursue new ambitions,
   D. retired, from football to pursue new ambitions,

Across the street from the <u>synagogue, we attend,</u> the soup kitchen is always open to feed anyone who is hungry.

2. F. NO CHANGE
   G. synagogue, we attend
   H. synagogue we attend
   J. synagogue we attend,

It is on a quiet street, <u>located; between</u> a large field on one side and a gas station on the other.

3. A. NO CHANGE
   B. located between,
   C. located, between
   D. located between

<u>So, researchers decided,</u> to look for the sunken vessel themselves.

4. F. NO CHANGE
   G. So researchers decided
   H. So researchers, decided
   J. So researchers decided,

In the world of epidemiology, scientists struggle to make generalizations about bacteria, which are sometimes <u>beneficial</u> sometimes harmful.

5. A. NO CHANGE
   B. beneficial,
   C. beneficial, and,
   D. beneficial:

Problem Set 10: Punctuation

The phone at the office rings at least twenty times

a <u>day</u> I feel like I have talked to every person in
  ₆

the town.

6. F. NO CHANGE
   G. day, although
   H. day actually
   J. day, and

Tretheway is the official Poet Laureate of both

the United States and <u>Mississippi, and she</u> has
                        ₇

also served as a distinguished professor at Emory

University.

7. Which of the following alternatives to the
   underlined portion would NOT be acceptable?
   A. Mississippi; she
   B. Mississippi. She
   C. Mississippi and
   D. Mississippi, she

Our E-mail inbox fills up with a mix of junk mail

and real <u>mail that we must</u> sort through and either
          ₈

respond to or delete.

8. F. NO CHANGE
   G. mail, these we must
   H. mail and we have to
   J. mail, we must

It is disconcerting to know that the <u>professor and</u>
                                      ₉

<u>that her</u> teaching assistants are always watching
₉

me take my exams.

9. A. NO CHANGE
   B. professor. Her
   C. professor and her
   D. professor. And her

Microsoft's <u>founder and chairman Bill Gates,</u>
              ₁₀

claims that people should be nice to nerds

because they will likely end up working for one.

10. F. NO CHANGE
    G. founder, and chairman Bill Gates,
    H. founder, and chairman Bill Gates
    J. founder and chairman, Bill Gates,

Problem Set 10: Punctuation

Cherokee Data Solutions also hires Native

American <u>professional technicians</u> and
          ₁₁

subcontractors whenever possible and contracts

Native Americans to script much of the code that

the company uses.

11. A. NO CHANGE
     B. professional, technicians,
     C. professional technicians;
     D. professional technicians,

If you wait long enough, sometimes you can get

lucky, and a program you thought was <u>frozen,</u>
                                 ₁₂

<u>will</u> inexplicably start working again.
₁₂

12. F. NO CHANGE
     G. frozen will
     H. frozen — will
     J. frozen; will

Suddenly, without warning, each of the <u>kittens in</u>
                                ₁₃

<u>front of you rolls</u> onto its back to ask for a
₁₃

bellyrub.

13. A. NO CHANGE
     B. kittens, in front of you rolls
     C. kittens in front of you rolls,
     D. kittens in front of you, rolls

Not all <u>boomerangs; however,</u> return themselves
          ₁₄

to the thrower.

14. F. NO CHANGE
     G. boomerangs however,
     H. boomerangs, however,
     J. boomerangs, however

Evidence that SUV manufacturers are playing up

the rugged image is found in the names of their

<u>vehicles;</u> Yukon, Xterra, Pathfinder, Excursion,
₁₅

and Tahoe.

15. A. NO CHANGE
     B. vehicles:
     C. vehicles
     D. vehicles,

Problem Set 10: Punctuation

My grandfather is not keen on embracing new technology. He still uses his old Motorola flip phone. He claims, he can't imagine using spiffy options like Internet or GPS.

16. F. NO CHANGE
    G. technology he still uses
    H. technology still using,
    J. technology, and still using

17. A. NO CHANGE
    B. claims that,
    C. claims, that,
    D. claims

The Phantom drone's user could control the position of the drone, and the angle of the camera, and the live video feed from the drone would show up on the user's smart phone. The GPS system on the drone keeps the drone in place automatically, which is very convenient when the user is focused on the camera.

18. F. NO CHANGE
    G. drone and, the angle,
    H. drone and the angle
    J. drone and the angle,

19. A. NO CHANGE
    B. convenient, when
    C. convenient. When
    D. convenient; when

Many of the moves from mambo and chacha were adopted by New York dancers, who began to refer to their style, as a new type of dance salsa.

20. F. NO CHANGE
    G. style as a new type of dance,
    H. style, as a new type of dance,
    J. style as a new type of dance

Eventually, Yadav wrote 'Capers, a play she developed; based on the stories of families who live in public housing.

21. A. NO CHANGE
    B. developed based, on
    C. developed based on
    D. developed based on,

Problem Set 10: Punctuation

Her fluency in the language allowed her to

achieve <u>success in the Russian-speaking regions</u>
                                        22

of Europe and Asia.

22. F. NO CHANGE
    G. success: in the Russian-speaking regions
    H. success, in the Russian-speaking regions,
    J. success in the Russian-speaking regions,

In an early morning meeting on June 5, <u>1944,</u>
                                              23

<u>Eisenhower</u> ordered the troops to proceed with
23

the following day's invasion.

23. A. NO CHANGE
    B. 1944, and Eisenhower
    C. 1944. Eisenhower
    D. 1944; Eisenhower

In 1857, <u>journalist and landscape architect</u>
                          24

Frederick Law Olmsted entered a contest to

design New York City's Central Park.

24. F. NO CHANGE
    G. journalist, and landscape architect
    H. journalist and landscape architect,
    J. journalist, and landscape architect,

The walls were lined with images of other

climbers—many of them <u>the heroes who had</u>
                                        25

<u>inspired me to pursue such</u> an arduous trek.
25

25. A. NO CHANGE
    B. the heroes who, had inspired me to pursue such
    C. the heroes, who had inspired me, to pursue such
    D. the heroes who had inspired me to pursue, such

That box contained all of my memories from my

trip to <u>Russia and unlike</u> my other travels, my
                    26

journey to Russia was very emotional.

26. F. NO CHANGE
    G. Russia unlike
    H. Russia, unlike
    J. Russia. Unlike

Problem Set 10: Punctuation

Usually in charge of most of the hunting for the

<u>pride, or group of,</u> lions, the lionesses are swifter
　　　27

and more agile than their male counterparts.

27.　A. NO CHANGE
　　　B. pride, or group, of
　　　C. pride or group of,
　　　D. pride or, group of

Though much remains to be discovered, what's

already <u>clear is, that</u> the great white shark is not
　　　　　28

the malicious, calculating killer portrayed in the

movie Jaws.

28.　F. NO CHANGE
　　　G. clear, is that
　　　H. clear is that
　　　J. clear is that,

The majority of sharks are <u>carnivores; the</u>
　　　　　　　　　　　　　29

<u>basking shark,</u> is a filter feeder, subsisting
　　　29

primarily on zooplankton.

29.　A. NO CHANGE
　　　B. carnivores, the basking shark
　　　C. carnivores so the basking shark
　　　D. carnivores; the basking shark

Once we've written and edited the script, <u>filming</u>
　　　　　　　　　　　　　　　　　　　30

<u>for the episode, begins.</u>
　　　30

30.　F. NO CHANGE
　　　G. filming for the episode begin.
　　　H. we begin, filming for the episode.
　　　J. filming for the episode begins.

Even though mountain <u>lions supposedly</u>
　　　　　　　　　　　　31

disappeared from Connecticut decades ago, one

was recently killed by a motorist in Milford. Many

<u>sightings, most of them reported by concerned</u>
　　　　　　　　　　　32

<u>citizens</u> have occurred across the state.
　32

31.　A. NO CHANGE
　　　B. lions, supposedly
　　　C. lions supposedly,
　　　D. lions' had supposedly

32.　F. NO CHANGE
　　　G. sightings—most of them reported by concerned citizens —
　　　H. sightings, having been reported by concerned citizens,
　　　J. sightings; most of them reported by concerned citizens,

Problem Set 10: Punctuation

In Cincinnati's Academy of World Languages

program, students are immersed in a <u>language,</u>
                                               33

<u>each</u> day, children take classes in Mandarin,
33

Russian, Japanese, and Arabic.

33. A. NO CHANGE
    B. language, and that each
    C. language and that each
    D. language. Each

<u>It's also dangerous,</u> motorcycle death rates
         34

increased 55 percent from 2001 to 2008.

34. F. NO CHANGE
    G. It's also dangerous:
    H. Its also dangerous,
    J. Its also dangerous;

The <u>one redeeming, feature of the Articles of</u>
                35

<u>Confederation</u> was that they provided a method
35

for assigning statehood to new territories.

35. A. NO CHANGE
    B. one, redeeming, feature of the Articles of
       Confederation
    C. one redeeming feature of the Articles of
       Confederation
    D. one redeeming feature of the Articles of
       Confederation,

This apparent violation of constitutional <u>rights is</u>
                       36

<u>the subject</u> of scholarly debate.
36

36. F. NO CHANGE
    G. rights, is the subject
    H. rights is the subject,
    J. rights: is the subject

Keys are then hammered out from iron <u>nails, and</u>
                           37

<u>the</u> board is sanded to perfection.
37

37. Which of the following alternatives to the
    underlined portion would NOT be acceptable?
    A. nails, while the
    B. nails, the
    C. nails; the
    D. nails. The

Perhaps the most notable aspect of African <u>mbira</u>
                                 38

<u>music</u> is that it is based on cross-rhythms.
38

38. F. NO CHANGE
    G. mbira music is,
    H. mbira, music, is
    J. mbira music is:

Problem Set 10: Punctuation

A rabbi in his robes, three businessmen in suits, and a team of basketball players in sharp, <u>royal blue track suits</u> wait in the security line.
   39
   39

39. A. NO CHANGE
    B. royal blue, track suits
    C. royal, blue track suits
    D. royal blue track suits,

This program, known by the government code name PRISM, has been in existence in the United States since 2007, <u>gathering data on:</u> electronic
   40
communications made by American citizens, foreign civilians, and even foreign governments.

40. F. NO CHANGE
    G. gathering data: on
    H. gathering data on
    J. gathering data, on

PRISM was enabled by the <u>passage of the Protect</u>
   41
<u>America Act,</u> of 2007.
   41

41. A. NO CHANGE
    B. passage of the Protect America Act
    C. passage, of the Protect America Act
    D. passage, of the protect America Act,

Outside of Snowden, such leaks have been <u>rare,</u>
   42
<u>which</u> made his discretion even more surprising.
   42

42. Which of the following alternatives to the underlined portion would NOT be acceptable?
    F. rare. This
    G. rare, a factor that
    H. rare; this
    J. rare, this

When renowned musician Trombone <u>Shorty,</u>
   43
<u>practices his craft</u> everybody listens.
   43

43. A. NO CHANGE
    B. Shorty, practices his craft,
    C. Shorty practices, his craft,
    D. Shorty practices his craft,

Problem Set 10: Punctuation

All along, Troy Andrews has been releasing

albums—from 2003's release as part of the

Stooges Brass Band to <u>Backatown, a</u> 2010 release

44

with his Orleans Avenue band that earned him a

nomination for a Grammy Award. Andrews began

to realize the extent of his popularity when

<u>guitarist Lenny Kravitz</u> who had won four

45

straight Grammy Awards from 1999 to 2002,

recruited Andrews for the brass section of his

2005 world tour with <u>Aerosmith that</u> was an

46

epiphany for Andrews.

Andrews began playing trombone in New

Orleans' brass band parades but has since played

a number of different <u>styles, jazz, rock, hip-hop,</u>

47

<u>blues,</u> (with legendary guitarist Eric Clapton),

47

funk (with fellow New Orleans natives Galactic).

If the key fails at first to hit the right note—like

most keys do—the <u>craftsman must be patient,</u>

48   48

<u>slowly hammering</u> the key into the correct shape.

44. F. NO CHANGE
    G. Backatown, this was a
    H. Backatown. A
    J. Backatown; a

45. A. NO CHANGE
    B. guitarist, Lenny Kravitz
    C. guitarist, Lenny Kravitz,
    D. guitarist Lenny Kravitz,

46. F. NO CHANGE
    G. Aerosmith. This
    H. Aerosmith,
    J. Aerosmith, this

47. A. NO CHANGE
    B. styles: jazz, rock, hip-hop, blues,
    C. styles, jazz, rock, hip-hop, blues
    D. styles: jazz, rock, hip-hop, blues

48. Which of the following alternatives to the underlined portion would NOT be acceptable?
    F. craftsman must patiently hammer
    G. craftsman, who must be patient, hammers
    H. craftsman, who must patiently hammer
    J. patient craftsman must hammer

Problem Set 10: Punctuation

Once the election is held, yearbook committee

members tally the votes over the course of a week

and <u>then, announce to the school</u> the winners of
49

the superlatives.

49. A. NO CHANGE
    B. then announce to the school
    C. then, announce, to the school
    D. then annouce to the school,

Dolphins, therefore, navigate the oceans by

means of <u>echolocation—the</u> use of calls and
50

echoes to locate and identify objects.

50. Which of the following alternatives to the underlined portion would NOT be acceptable?
    F. echolocation, the
    G. echolocation: the
    H. echolocation, which is the
    J. echolocation. The

The patient now has a filled-in, complete <u>beard.</u>
51

<u>Eventually, it</u> will grow in as thick as a normal
51

beard, although up to ten months are necessary to

see the full result.

51. Which of the following alternatives to the underlined portion would NOT be acceptable?
    A. beard, eventually, it
    B. beard that eventually
    C. beard, which eventually
    D. beard; eventually, it

The next improvement project <u>was to fix,</u> up the
52

barn that once had been home to two horses.

52. F. NO CHANGE
    G. was, to fix
    H. was to fix
    J. was: to fix

Neither of the motorcycles was working properly,

but at least the <u>engines the hearts of the bikes,</u>
53

were in good condition.

53. A. NO CHANGE
    B. engines: the hearts of the bikes
    C. engines, the hearts of the bikes,
    D. engines, the hearts of the bikes

Problem Set 10: Punctuation

The rambunctious <u>kittens also</u> led me to ask
₅₄
another question: what is life without time to

play?

54. F. NO CHANGE
    G. kitten's also
    H. kittens also,
    J. kittens, also

George Lucas' career in film took off after he was

featured as <u>producer; and director</u> of the film *Star*
₅₅

Wars: Episode IV - A New Hope.

55. A. NO CHANGE
    B. producer, and director
    C. producer and director,
    D. producer and director

Lucas <u>says, that</u> if you can tune into the fantasy
₅₆
life of an eleven-year-old girl, you can make a

fortune in the movie business.

56. F. NO CHANGE
    G. says that
    H. says: that
    J. says; that

One writer who did publish in the early 1900s,

Franz <u>Kafka, who</u> would have been forgotten
₅₇

were it not for his good friend Max Brod, who

published Kafka's work against his wishes after

the author's death.

57. A. NO CHANGE
    B. Kafka,
    C. Kafka. He
    D. Kafka;

Harper Lee's only surviving works were *To Kill a*

Mockingbird <u>and, a handful of, magazine articles</u>
₅₈

that were published in various periodicals.

58. F. NO CHANGE
    G. *Mockingbird* and a handful of magazine articles,
    H. *Mockingbird*, and a handful of magazine articles
    J. *Mockingbird* and a handful of magazine articles

Problem Set 10: Punctuation

Legend has it that Sitting Bull led the Cheyenne and Lakota forces in the Battle of Little Big Horn in <u>1876; when</u> the Native Americans were
₅₉
attacked by General Custer's troops, but Sitting Bull did not actually play a direct military role in the battle.

59. A. NO CHANGE
    B. 1876: when
    C. 1876 when
    D. 1876. When

It's considered an <u>unusual choice, but celebrity</u>
₆₀
<u>chef Gordon Ramsey</u> decided to include thyme in
₆₀
his cookies.

60. F. NO CHANGE
    G. unusual choice but celebrity chef, Gordon Ramsey,
    H. unusual choice, but celebrity chef, Gordon Ramsey,
    J. unusual choice, but celebrity chef Gordon Ramsey,

The official flag of Peru features just two <u>colors,</u>
₆₁
<u>white and red,</u> representing peace and the blood
₆₁
spilled in the struggle for independence.

61. A. NO CHANGE
    B. colors white and red,
    C. colors, white and red
    D. colors, white, and red,

The flag of Belize features a detailed image of two men holding logging <u>tools for example,</u>
₆₂
<u>while</u> the flag of England bears a simple red cross
₆₂
on a white background.

62. F. NO CHANGE
    G. tools, for example while
    H. tools, for example, while
    J. tools, for example,

Problem Set 10: Punctuation

The gymnast dismounted the balance <u>beam, many</u>
63

viewers held their breaths to see if she would stick

the landing.

63. A. NO CHANGE
    B. beam many
    C. beam. Many
    D. beam. While many

Growing <u>up, in Egypt in 100 C.E.</u> Ptolemy
64

believed the earth was the center of the universe.

64. F. NO CHANGE
    G. up in Egypt in 100 C.E.,
    H. up, in Egypt in 100 C.E.,
    J. up in Egypt, in 100 C.E.,

Mayor LaGuardia built a performing arts high

school and hired some of the top artists to instruct

students <u>in: dance</u> and theater.
65

65. A. NO CHANGE
    B. in, dance
    C. in dance
    D. in dance,

Though Edwin Hubble died in 1953, his <u>legacy:</u>
66

the Hubble Space Telescope—lives on, a valuable

contribution to science.

66. F. NO CHANGE
    G. legacy,
    H. legacy—
    J. legacy

This is not a deliberate <u>act, which</u> I just
67

unconsciously assume people like getting their

hair stroked.

67. A. NO CHANGE
    B. act that
    C. act.
    D. act

Problem Set 10: Punctuation

Small piles of dust <u>gather</u> as if of their own
₆₈

accord, in the corners of my basement.

68. F. NO CHANGE
    G. gather;
    H. gather,
    J. gather:

For instance, at a <u>speed of sixty miles per hour.</u>
₆₉

<u>Drivers</u> travel eighty-eight feet per second.
₆₉

69. A. NO CHANGE
    B. speed, of sixty miles per hour, drivers
    C. speed of sixty miles per hour; drivers
    D. speed of sixty miles per hour, drivers

Writing bills would take much longer if every

draft had to be retyped from <u>scratch, using</u>
₇₀

<u>computers</u> really revolutionized our legislative
₇₀

system.

70. F. NO CHANGE
    G. scratch using computers
    H. scratch using computers,
    J. scratch. Using computers

Eli Whitney's <u>contributions to cotton farming</u> and
₇₁

his work in gun production may seem to be an

unlikely pairing.

71. A. NO CHANGE
    B. contributions, to cotton farming,
    C. contributions, to cotton farming
    D. contributions to cotton farming,

A world-class <u>oncologist:</u> he is best remembered for
₇₂

the care and attention he brought to every patient.

72. F. NO CHANGE
    G. oncologist;
    H. oncologist,
    J. oncologist

Problem Set 10: Punctuation

In 1998, the year our house was <u>built. NASA</u> was

building a house in low orbit around the earth: the

International Space Station.

73. A. NO CHANGE
    B. built NASA
    C. built, NASA
    D. built; NASA

Report cards must now be mailed to students'

<u>houses. What</u> was once posted on a bulletin board

for public viewing is now considered private,

sensitive material.

74. Which of the following alternatives to the underlined
    portion would NOT be acceptable?
    F. houses, so that what
    G. houses; what
    H. houses, what
    J. houses: what

My cat is impossible not to <u>love</u> her little

whiskers, long white fur, and the sound of her

purring when she's happy.

75. A. NO CHANGE
    B. love:
    C. love,
    D. love;

My <u>fascination with killer whales,</u> put me into

some interesting situations.

76. F. NO CHANGE
    G. fascination, with killer whales
    H. fascination with killer whales
    J. fascination, with killer whales,

We could now <u>hear, the boom and howl</u> of an

incoming thunderstorm.

77. A. NO CHANGE
    B. hear the boom, and howl
    C. hear the boom and howl,
    D. hear the boom and howl

Problem Set 10: Punctuation

On my way to JFK Airport, I became friends with

a <u>taxi driver, named</u> Lou.
₇₈

78. F. NO CHANGE
    G. taxi driver; named
    H. taxi driver named
    J. taxi, driver, named

I had no experience with <u>women when</u> I had
₇₉

always been too scared to talk to them.

79. A. NO CHANGE
    B. women, when
    C. women;
    D. women, however,

The skydiving instructor had a pleasant smile on

his <u>face, I think,</u> she could tell how scared I was.
₈₀

80. F. NO CHANGE
    G. face I think
    H. face. I think
    J. face, however, I think

I watched him gently nudge Katie's <u>shoulder,</u>
₈₁

<u>which she</u> jolted awake.
₈₁

81. A. NO CHANGE
    B. shoulder, which it
    C. shoulder. She
    D. shoulder, where she

The walking catfish can spend days roaming on

top of dry <u>land; thus</u> helping them survive extreme
₈₂

drought.

82. F. NO CHANGE
    G. water and thus
    H. water, thus
    J. water. Thus

Problem Set 10: Punctuation

The school has a zero tolerance policy for those

<u>who bully or harass</u> other students.
     83

83. A. NO CHANGE
    B. who bully, or harass
    C. who bully or harass,
    D. who, bully or harass,

The new technology will reduce the carbon

emissions of automobiles and commercial <u>trucks,</u>
                         84

<u>of</u> small speedboats and cruise ships.
84

84. F. NO CHANGE
    G. trucks;
    H. trucks and,
    J. trucks of

The communal nature of travel has given me the

opportunity to meet people of all ethnicities and

religions who share my <u>philosophy that is</u> travel
                          85

alone, live simply, and discover the world.

85. A. NO CHANGE
    B. philosophy being
    C. philosophy:
    D. philosophy

The air was cold and <u>clear, the stars</u> spectacular
                       86

against the black sky.

86. Which of the following alternatives to the
    underlined portion would NOT be acceptable?
    F. clear; the stars looked
    G. clear. The stars were
    H. clear; the stars that were looking
    J. clear, and the stars were

Problem Set 10: Punctuation

"Megan, there's The Big Dipper," Dad said,

he kneeled so I could spot the unmistakable

arrangement of stars, perfectly <u>aligned, at the end,</u>

87

of his pointing finger.

87. A. NO CHANGE
    B. aligned; at the end
    C. aligned at the end,
    D. aligned, at the end

These days, with authors writing up to five articles

a <u>year; it's</u> easy to forget that at one time writing

88

multiple articles a year was rare.

88. F. NO CHANGE
    G. year, it's
    H. year; its
    J. year, its

David Snyder was the first Olympian to win three

bronze <u>medals, placing</u> third in the steeplechase,

89

the hurdles, and the 200-meter dash.

89. A. NO CHANGE
    B. medals; placing
    C. medals, he placed
    D. medals, placed

As a result, Snyder no long <u>needed his:</u> glasses,

90

monocle, or contact lenses after the surgery.

90. F. NO CHANGE
    G. needed his
    H. needed the following: his
    J. needed, his

During his junior <u>year, Ed Lewandowski,</u> Yale's

91

debate captain, noticed that Snyder might have

some ability as a politician.

91. A. NO CHANGE
    B. year Ed Lewandowski
    C. year, Ed Lewandowski
    D. year, Ed Lewandowski-

Problem Set 10: Punctuation

<u>Snyder was aware</u> that his high school didn't have
92

a fencing team, Lewandowski invited Snyder to

attend a summer sports camp in the mountains.

92. F. NO CHANGE
    G. Snyder, who was
    H. Snyder, aware
    J. Aware

With their help, Snyder attended college on a

debate scholarship and competed with the world

renowned Yale debate <u>team then he moved</u> to New
93

York City where he worked for a top law firm.

93. A. NO CHANGE
    B. team: then moving
    C. team before moving
    D. team; before he moved

He made the Republican Debate, and in Hanover,

<u>New Hampshire. He</u> destroyed his opponents.
94

94. F. NO CHANGE
    G. New Hampshire: He
    H. New Hampshire; he
    J. New Hampshire, he

Imagine a cross between a graceful figure skater

and a rugged football player, <u>you</u> will have some
95

idea of the surprising traits of this lone explorer -

the mountain goat.

95. A. NO CHANGE
    B. if so, you
    C. and
    D. and you

The hulking beast <u>routinely travels up</u> and down
96

nearly vertical rock faces with great skill and

apparently no fear.

96. F. NO CHANGE
    G. routinely, travels up
    H. routinely, travels, up
    J. routinely travels up,

Problem Set 10: Punctuation

Goat species that <u>travel extensively</u> have thick
  97
wool that protects the goat at times like these.

97. A. NO CHANGE
    B. travel; extensively,
    C. travel extensively,
    D. travel, extensively

In other words, the goat is outfitted with the
outdoor <u>jacket needed, to execute the tasks,</u>
  98
required for survival.

98. F. NO CHANGE
    G. jacket needed to execute the tasks,
    H. jacket needed to execute the tasks
    J. jacket, needed to perform the tasks

With <u>fellow, writer,</u> Bob Steinhardt, Johnson
  99
helped finish the book in two months.

99. A. NO CHANGE
    B. fellow writer
    C. fellow writer,
    D. fellow, writer

The <u>result</u> in this instance and others, is language
  100
that creates visuals and tells a uniquely compelling
narrative.

100. F. NO CHANGE
     G. result-
     H. result,
     J. result is

Coleman was also friends with many workers
back <u>home and many</u> workers had the skillset
  101
to contribute to New York but couldn't afford to
emigrate.

101. A. NO CHANGE
     B. home many
     C. home. Many
     D. home, many

Problem Set 10: Punctuation

He persuaded three of his friends to move from

Ireland to <u>Brooklyn to</u> help in his attempt to build
　　　　　　　102

a restaurant.

102. F. NO CHANGE
     G. Brooklyn; to
     H. Brooklyn. To
     J. Brooklyn. In order to

Yellowstone National Forest in Wyoming

has highly varied landscape—rivers, valleys,

mountains, plains—and constitutes a home for an

array of animals that <u>includes:</u> wolves, buffalos,
　　　　　　　　　　　　103

hares, and some 25 kinds of fish.

103. A. NO CHANGE
     B. includes
     C. includes,
     D. includes the following,

He affectionately jokes that studying the wild

wolves, which he often does for hours at a <u>time is</u>
　　　　　　　　　　　　　　　　　　　　　104

<u>like watching</u> a reality TV show.
　　104

104. F. NO CHANGE
     G. time, is like watching,
     H. time, is like watching
     J. time is like watching,

During the summer, Raul films each of the wolf

packs on his digital <u>camera, he does so</u> throughout
　　　　　　　　　　　　105

the day as he talks with other scientists, explaining

to them the intricacies of each unique pack.

105. A. NO CHANGE
     B. camera,
     C. camera
     D. camera it happens

Problem Set 10: Punctuation

That same year, <u>1955,</u> the producer encouraged
₁₀₆

<u>Schulman, then twenty-two,</u> to start acting in
₁₀₇

films.

106. F. NO CHANGE
    G. 1955
    H. 1955;
    J. 1955, and

107. Which of the following alternatives to the underlined portion would NOT be acceptable?
    A. Schulman—then twenty-two—
    B. Schulman, who was twenty-two,
    C. Schulman, twenty-two,
    D. Schulman, then twenty-two

James North opened <u>his skateboard shop Bones in</u>
₁₀₈

<u>1987</u> with just 50 dollars to his name.
₁₀₈

108. F. NO CHANGE
    G. his, skateboard shop, Bones in 1987,
    H. his skateboard shop: Bones, in 1987
    J. his, skateboard shop Bones, in 1987

His goal was to channel the surfing vibe of the

<u>1960s.</u> California lifestyle of which he had been a
₁₀₉

part.

109. A. NO CHANGE
    B. 1960s;
    C. 1960s,
    D. 1960s

North's plan relied on using young, cool teens from

his <u>neighborhood. Because</u> he hoped their fresh
₁₁₀

vibe would create a brand new cult movement

around skateboard culture.

110. F. NO CHANGE
    G. neighborhood because
    H. neighborhood—because
    J. neighborhood; because

Problem Set 10: Punctuation

In 1990, in an attempt to save the store, North

moved it to a new location with a new <u>partner,</u>
₁₁₁

<u>Andrew Wexler,</u> wanted the store to reflect a more
₁₁₁

grunge aesthetic.

111. A. NO CHANGE
    B. partner. Andrew Wexler
    C. partner—Andrew Wexler—
    D. partner Andrew Wexler

For a period, the store's <u>survival was uncertain.</u>
₁₁₂

<u>In fact,</u> its doors were closed for six months while
₁₁₂

Wexler raised capital and renovated.

112. F. NO CHANGE
    G. survival was uncertain. In fact;
    H. survival was uncertain in fact
    J. survival was uncertain—in fact

Visitors can view a collection of rare meteor

samples and taxidermy animals <u>shot,</u> by former
₁₁₃

President Theodore Roosevelt in the early 1900s.

113. A. NO CHANGE
    B. shoot,
    C. shot
    D. shoot

After all, these rooms are only a small portion of

the collection of biological exhibits and an even

smaller <u>portion, of the museum's</u> total collection.
₁₁₄

114. F. NO CHANGE
    G. portion of the museums
    H. portion of the museum's
    J. portion of the museums,

The organic farming exhibit at the museum stores

all of its <u>live animals in the Webster Center; in the</u>
₁₁₅

Biotic Wing of the museum.

115. A. NO CHANGE
    B. live animals in the Webster Center
    C. live animals, in the Webster Center;
    D. live animals, in the Webster Center

Problem Set 10: Punctuation

Any member can simply meander through and look at the specimens organized by <u>habitat such as,</u> desert, forest, tundra, and plain.
₁₁₆

116. F. NO CHANGE
G. habitat; such as
H. habitat, such as
J. habitat, such as,

Climatically appropriate <u>habitats, at the museum</u> allow the animals to feel comfortable while serving as a learning tool for visitors.
₁₁₇

117. A. NO CHANGE
B. habitats at the museum
C. habitats, at the museum,
D. habitats at the museum,

Jesse Kolber even fudges his date of <u>birth, he falsely lists</u> 1998 so people think he's a teenager.
₁₁₈

118. F. NO CHANGE
G. birth; he falsely lists
H. birth; falsely listing
J. birth, falsely listing:

Jesse's attempts to convince people he's a teenager—whether deliberate affectations or lack of awareness—ultimately matter very <u>little, for</u> no one is ever fooled.
₁₁₉

119. A. NO CHANGE
B. little. For
C. little; for
D. little,

The moniker "babyface" was conferred upon Roger Reiersen by his cohorts at Boston University. <u>He himself,</u> adopted the name and, subsequently, a corresponding persona.
₁₂₀

120. F. NO CHANGE
G. He, himself,
H. He, himself
J. He himself

Problem Set 10: Punctuation

Over the centuries, different cultures have used different methods for making <u>bread, each</u> culture
121
has used two essential ingredients: grain and yeast.

121. A. NO CHANGE
    B. bread, each and every
    C. bread that each
    D. bread, but each

Patents emerged for <u>newly designed</u> washing
122
machines settings intended exclusively for difficult-to-wash attire, like silk ties and wool sweaters.

122. F. NO CHANGE
    G. newly designed,
    H. newly, designed
    J. newly, designed,

Magellan was selected by King Charles I of Spain to lead <u>a newly formed group of young sailors</u> and
123
travel west to reach the Indies.

123. A. NO CHANGE
    B. a, newly formed, group of young sailors
    C. a newly, formed group of young sailors
    D. a newly formed, group of young sailors,

Throughout his travels, Lars would meticulously describe, in writing and through pictures, each exotic fruit he tried, <u>including: details about how it</u>
124
tasted, smelled, looked, and felt.

124. F. NO CHANGE
    G. including details about how it:
    H. including details about: how it
    J. including details about how it

Problem Set 10: Punctuation

When Coursera became popular in the last decade, people were excited about its goal making ₁₂₅ videotaped college-level courses available to the general public.

125. A. NO CHANGE
   B. goal: making
   C. goal. To make
   D. goal. Making

IKEA strives to preserve its original goal, of ₁₂₆ making cost-effective yet durable furniture, for all ₁₂₆ kinds of shoppers.

126. F. NO CHANGE
   G. goal, of making cost-effective yet durable furniture
   H. goal of making cost effective yet durable furniture,
   J. goal of making cost-effective yet durable furniture

When conducting deep ocean tours, scuba divers must be vigilant that tourists don't resurface too ₁₂₇ quickly.

127. A. NO CHANGE
   B. vigilant. That
   C. vigilant, that
   D. vigilant that,

The Statue of Liberty became a symbol both of the ₁₂₈ American dream, of modernism, and the rise of ₁₂₈ New York City.

128. F. NO CHANGE
   G. both of the American dream, and
   H. of: the American dream,
   J. of the American dream,

Though some tourists at the Great Wall of China ₁₂₉ paused to take pictures, the length of the wall reinforced my desire to keep moving.

129. A. NO CHANGE
   B. some—tourists at the Great Wall of China
   C. some, tourists at the Great Wall of China
   D. some tourists, at the Great Wall of China

Problem Set 10: Punctuation

Called a "superconductor" because it is highly conductive at low <u>temperatures—silver</u> is the
₁₃₀
most electrically conductive element in the universe.

130. F. NO CHANGE
    G. temperatures;
    H. temperatures,
    J. temperatures

For years, <u>though Dmitry Budker of UC Berkeley,</u> has been working to develop portable MRI
₁₃₁
machines at a low cost.

131. A. NO CHANGE
    B. though, Dmitry Budker of UC Berkeley
    C. though, Dmitry Budker, of UC Berkeley
    D. though Dmitry Budker, of UC Berkeley

'Trap crops,' which are planted to divert <u>bugs</u>
₁₂₈
<u>away, from other plants</u> are particularly helpful for
₁₂₈
organic farmers, who must find a way to stop using great quantities of harmful pesticides.

132. F. NO CHANGE
    G. bugs away, from other plants,
    H. bugs away from other plants,
    J. bugs away from other plants

The noises were mostly <u>mechanical—we lived for</u>
₁₃₃
<u>most of my childhood</u> right above a car repair shop.
₁₃₃

133. Which of the following would NOT be an acceptable replacement?
    A. mechanical; we lived for most of my childhood
    B. mechanical, we lived for most of my childhood
    C. mechanical. We lived for most of my childhood
    D. mechanical; for most of my childhood, we lived

Problem Set 10: Punctuation

Baseball games that start late can sometimes <u>last</u>
₁₃₄

<u>long past</u> midnight.
₁₃₄

134. F. NO CHANGE
    G. last long, past,
    H. last, long past,
    J. last, long past

Around this time, people who recently moved into

the <u>cities;</u> left their mark.
₁₃₅

135. A. NO CHANGE
    B. cities
    C. cities:
    D. cities,

To add to <u>the confusion, I often</u> didn't know how to
₁₃₆

answer her questions.

136. F. NO CHANGE
    G. confusion, I often,
    H. confusion, I often;
    J. confusion I often,

<u>The Administrative Board;</u> agreed to listen to the
₁₃₇

students' appeal.

137. A. NO CHANGE
    B. The Administrative Board
    C. The Administrative Board,
    D. The Administrative, Board

Marines live together in barracks with bunks, a

shower and toilet, a television, and an array of

movies to watch. Sailors could navigate the seas

from the <u>*poop deck,* an</u> elevated observation deck
₁₃₈

located at a ship's stern.

138. F. NO CHANGE
    G. *poop deck.* An
    H. *poop deck*; an
    J. *poop deck* an

Problem Set 10: Punctuation

Johnson similarly utilized different power tools,

<u>these can be</u> drills and nail guns, as well as saws
₁₃₉

and power sanders.

139. A. NO CHANGE
    B. these include
    C. such as
    D. two examples are

On either side of her is a <u>child that the mother</u>
₁₄₀

<u>holds</u> her children's hands as they cross the street.
₁₄₀

140. F. NO CHANGE
    G. child; the mother holds
    H. child the mother holds
    J. child that the mother is holding

Rainbow patterns appear on puddles when a drop

of oil <u>hits the water's surface it causes</u> the oil
₁₄₁

molecules to spread into a monolayer.

141. A. NO CHANGE
    B. hits the water's surface, causing
    C. hits the water's surface, it causes
    D. hits the water's surface, this causes

It's not uncommon for overconfident chefs to

experiment too <u>much, sometimes they</u> make
₁₄₂

mistakes cooking with ingredients they have never

used.

142. F. NO CHANGE
    G. much
    H. much or
    J. much sometimes they

The <u>bird itself</u> is a native of the Baltic states in
₁₄₃

northern Europe.

143. A. NO CHANGE
    B. bird, itself,
    C. bird, itself
    D. bird itself,

Problem Set 10: Punctuation

"Megan, there's The Big Dipper," Dad said,

<u>he kneeled</u> so I could spot the unmistakable

144

arrangement of stars.

144. F. NO CHANGE
    G. started to kneel
    H. kneeling
    J. and having kneeled

As we neared the finish line, the whole group of

bikers—thinly spread across the route for most of

the race—condensed, <u>forming</u> a tight pack across

                145

the road.

145. A. NO CHANGE
    B. they formed
    C. there was
    D. we saw

Redundancy

Avoid repeating any information in a sentence. The ACT loves to test redundancy by having three answer choices that all look similar and seem grammatically correct. Choose the right answer by cutting out the repetitive information.

Examples

Incorrect:
Each year, the American Red Cross responds to 70,000 disasters annually.

Correct:
Each year, the American Red Cross responds to 70,000 disasters.

2019-1

Problem Set 11: Redundancy

The design of the new flag presented a <u>problem, which needed a solution.</u>
₁

1. A. NO CHANGE
    B. problem, which was quite a dilemma.
    C. problem.
    D. problem that needed to be solved.

Old signs are still posted around the outside threatening punishment for potential <u>trespassers.</u>
₂

2. F. NO CHANGE
    G. trespassers who wrongfully enter the property.
    H. trespassers walking on private property.
    J. trespassers who ignore the signs.

Following graduation from high school, Miles Davis moved to New York to study at the <u>famed and notable</u> Juilliard School of Music.
₃

3. A. NO CHANGE
    B. prestigiously renowned
    C. delectable
    D. acclaimed

<u>At the outset, the original Netflix</u> first launched with just 30 employees and 925 works available for rent.
₄

4. F. NO CHANGE
    G. Netflix
    H. It was originally
    J. Initially, Netflix was

The weather threatened to postpone <u>and delay</u> the invasion of Normandy by at least two weeks.
₅

5. A. NO CHANGE
    B. to a later date
    C. and hold up
    D. OMIT the underlined portion

Over <u>two decades amounting to more than twenty years</u> of design and construction had finally concluded, and the longest suspension bridge in the world was now complete.
₆

6. F. NO CHANGE
    G. decades and more than twenty years
    H. decades—more than twenty years—
    J. decades

Problem Set 11: Redundancy

Regularly, common maladies, such as fever or

inflammation, were often treated with

bloodletting:eeches or sharp instruments were

used todraw blood from the patient.

7. A. NO CHANGE
   B. Common
   C. Quite frequently, common
   D. On many occasions, common

The producers agree that every episode has to be

funny and has to reflect and demonstrate the
                                            8

varied diversity of the actors involved.
       8

8. F. NO CHANGE
   G. reflect and mirror the diverse array of
   H. demonstrate the cultural diversity of the
   J. reflect the cultural diversity of the
      multicultural

Sudoku games are designed so that your main

opponent in these sudoku games is yourself, but
                                9

that hasn't stopped people from making sudoku

tournaments.

9. A. NO CHANGE
   B. during these games
   C. in sudoku games
   D. OMIT the underlined portion

No matter how many sudoku puzzles you solve,

the various setup of each game is always different
                          10

since there are 6,670,903,752,021,072,936,960

different grid solutions for the standard 9x9

puzzle.

10. F. NO CHANGE
    G. each
    H. each and every
    J. each single unique

Problem Set 11: Redundancy

Termites can permanently damage wood, and that

can be <u>disastrous for the structure</u> of the house.

11

11. A. NO CHANGE
    B. possibly disastrous to the structuring
    C. devestation for the structuring
    D. devestatingly disastrous for the structure

<u>Cleaning robots</u> are available that search for and

12

then remove any dirt from the floor.

12. F. NO CHANGE
    G. Cleaning robots that target dirt
    H. Dirt can be handled by cleaning robots that
    J. Cleaning robots that vacuum dirt

At the end of the meal, the waitress brought out a

large, <u>round cherry-covered bowl</u> of ice cream.

13

13. A. NO CHANGE
    B. massive cherry-covered bowl
    C. cherry-covered bowl
    D. fruit-coated, cherry-covered bowl

Fleming suspected that this staph-killing fungus

<u>may or may not provide</u> essential insight into

14

how to control bacterial infections.

14. F. NO CHANGE
    G. could provide valuable
    H. could very well provide one with
    J. might provide

Each day students learn new words and phrases

on which <u>eventually</u> the students will later be

15

tested.

15. A. NO CHANGE
    B. at some point in the future
    C. soon enough
    D. OMIT the underlined portion

The aspect of my trip that stands out the most in

my memory is the railway known as the

Shinkansen, whose bullet trains seem to testify to

the <u>frenzied and hectic pace of modern</u> life.

16

16. F. NO CHANGE
    G. franticness of modern contemporary
    H. baffled bewilderment of modern
    J. hectic pace of modern

Problem Set 11: Redundancy

There were so many things to consider when the puppies started crying. Were they famished? Hungry? Exhausted? Needing to go outside?
17

17. A. NO CHANGE
    B. Fatigued?
    C. Starving?
    D. OMIT the underlined portion

Many doctors and health policy experts warn that the recent boom in dietary supplements—
18
unregulated by the Food and Drug Administration—has come with hidden costs.

18. F. NO CHANGE
    G. supplements in the past few years
    H. supplements lately
    J. supplements just recently

There are over four hundred different species of shark, and I think perhaps I maybe possibly have
19
studied them all.

19. A. NO CHANGE
    B. I have
    C. I've maybe
    D. I have possibly

The movie tells the tale of Captain Richard
20
Phillips, who was the captain of the MV Maersk Alabama when it was hijacked by Somali pirates.

20. F. NO CHANGE
    G. movie, which tells a tale, is about
    H. movie chronicles and accounts for the story of
    J. movie is a film about

Olivia was persistent. Despite this, her parents acquiesced, when he thought about it and gave in,
21
allowing, even helping, her throw an after-prom party.

21. A. NO CHANGE
    B. in that he gave in,
    C. by finally agreeing,
    D. OMIT the underlined portion

Problem Set 11: Redundancy

Astronaut Neil <u>Armstrong, exploring outer space,</u> predicted that one day humans would be free to live and work on the moon.

22. F. NO CHANGE
    G. Armstrong—exploring outer space—
    H. Armstrong who explored outer space
    J. Armstrong

Eli Whitney is best known today for the <u>invention</u> and <u>creation</u> of the cotton 'gin.

23. A. NO CHANGE
    B. invention, which was the creation
    C. invention, that is, the creation,
    D. invention

In both situations, Ellery recognized <u>a need</u> and focused his creativity and determination to filling it.

24. F. NO CHANGE
    G. a lack of something that was needed
    H. that a need was in existence
    J. a need that was out there

First, <u>since he came from the South,</u> Faulkner's novels of a small town provide rare and valuable record of the daily life of Americans in Mississippi.

25. A. NO CHANGE
    B. because he is from Dixie,
    C. being that he has preserved the American South
    D. OMIT the underlined portion

One literary critic notes that Faulkner found it <u>completely natural</u> to write such long, complex sentences.

26. F. NO CHANGE
    G. totally free and easy
    H. to be his accustomed activity
    J. to be his usual and customary practice

Problem Set 11: Redundancy

For his livelihood, he waited tables for a living,
₂₇

but he most enjoyed the long, magnificent nights

he spent playing trumpet at the jazz club.

27. A. NO CHANGE
    B. He had started up waiting
    C. His livelihood was waiting
    D. He waited

At first, I was panicked like a siren blaring in my
₂₈

mind, but then my fear subsided.
₂₈

28. F. NO CHANGE
    G. panicked with fear and distress
    H. panicked by the sense of danger,
    J. panicked,

My instructor sat in the passenger seat as I

changed lanes on the highway for the first time. I

wasn't an expert driver, but at least I was an easy
₂₉

one to teach.

29. A. NO CHANGE
    B. a driver who drove with great skill or technique
    C. a master of the art of lane-changing,
    D. an expert,

It is interesting that although tomatoes are one

of the most abundant foods in Europe, they were

virtually absent from and nonexistent in 18th
₃₀

century cooking because people thought they were

poisonous.

30. F. NO CHANGE
    G. absent from
    H. not only absent from but also nonexistent in
    J. absent and not present in

The judge believes the witness's account is the
₃₁

likely story.
₃₁

31. A. NO CHANGE
    B. in all probability the likely
    C. likely the most probable
    D. very probably the likely

Problem Set 11: Redundancy

<u>Advocates supporting</u> limits on carbon usage
₃₂

often do not know how much they use themselves.

32. F. NO CHANGE
    G. Advocates who are in favor of
    H. Advocates of
    J. People who advocate and support

You can often use their kitchen, which provides an

alternative to costly <u>and expensive</u> dinners out on
₃₃

the town.

33. A. NO CHANGE
    B. and high-priced
    C. and pricey
    D. DELETE the underlined portion

He pointed out The Big Dipper to me, the

first constellation I would know, <u>the first</u>
₃₄

<u>commencement of a</u> beginning of a lifelong love
₃₄

affair with the stars.

34. F. NO CHANGE
    G. the initial
    H. the
    J. DELETE the underlined portion

Then came Ursa Minor, a smaller dipper that

created a tiny smudge of <u>noticeable light</u> above
₃₅

overhead.

35. A. NO CHANGE
    B. light
    C. light that looked something like a bight
       smear
    D. visible light that was there

I live in a city now, but last night I was at my

cousins' house in the suburbs, and I again went

outside <u>one more time again</u> to gaze at the clear
₃₆

night sky.

36. F. NO CHANGE
    G. one more time, again,
    H. once again
    J. DELETE the underlined portion

Problem Set 11: Redundancy

During the tournament, Ed Lewandowski, Yale's debate coach, <u>noticed that Snyder might possibly</u> <u>have some ability maybe</u> as a politician.
₃₇

37. A. NO CHANGE
    B. saw Snyder's ability to shine and excel
    C. noticed Snyder's potential
    D. observed that Snyder displayed some signs of possible potential ability

This thick skull protects the goat's brain from <u>damaging harm</u> when fighting other males.
₃₈

38. F. NO CHANGE
    G. damage
    H. harmful damage
    J. damage that can harm it

A keen sense of smell contributes to the goat's ability to locate grass, bark, berries, shrubs, and other plant foods <u>are located.</u>
₃₉

39. A. NO CHANGE
    B. make up its diet.
    C. are located by the Mountain Goat.
    D. DELETE the underlined portion and end the sentence with a period

Often the literature even seems to influence the <u>sounds that a listener can hear.</u>
₄₀

40. F. NO CHANGE
    G. sounds heard.
    H. aspects that are auditory in nature.
    J. sounds.

Every spring, <u>as they prepare for the summer</u>
₄₁
<u>season,</u> thousands of hungry wolves begin feasting
₄₁
in preparation of giving birth during the summer.

41. A. NO CHANGE
    B. needing to prepare for the season
    C. after starting to give birth in the summer
    D. DELETE the underlined portion

Problem Set 11: Redundancy

Information about each specimen is accessible <u>in the Webster Center</u> on touch screens in the center.

42. F. NO CHANGE
   G. for visitors to access
   H. to obtain
   J. DELETE the underlined portion

We tried to steady our canoe by redistributing our weight, but we capsized <u>because our weight was distributed unevenly.</u>

43. A. NO CHANGE
   B. even though we redistributed our weight.
   C. despite any efforts to even the canoe's weight.
   D. in a matter of seconds.

Colorful murals lighten the school's gray concrete structure. In every classroom, a Smart Board spans the width of the <u>gray</u> walls.

44. F. NO CHANGE
   G. gray concrete
   H. concrete
   J. DELETE the underlined portion

In keeping with the Cathedral's elaborate style, hand-carved wooden pews embrace the stage. Churchgoers credit the traditional Romanesque style with <u>adding enhancement to</u> their experience.

45. A. NO CHANGE
   B. adding enhancement to the experience of
   C. enhancing the experience of
   D. enhancing

Problem Set 11: Redundancy

Of the numerous early car inventors, <u>of which</u>
 46

<u>there were many,</u> Henry Ford is credited by most
 46

history textbooks with turning the tide against

horse-drawn carriages.

46. F. NO CHANGE
 G. who spent their time coming up with new machines,
 H. invention being a good thing,
 J. DELETE the underlined portion

Non-competitive sports like hiking and rock-

climbing can continue to foster <u>maximum</u>
 47

<u>enjoyment</u> with minimum bitterness and hard
 47

feelings.

47. A. NO CHANGE
 B. the most maximum enjoyment
 C. the most maximum enjoyment and pleasure
 D. maximum enjoyment and pleasure

Shortly after its completion in 2006, <u>the recently</u>
 48

<u>completed</u> High Line became one of New York's
 48

biggest tourist attractions.

48. F. NO CHANGE
 G. around that time, the
 H. soon thereafter, the
 J. the

Tourists took pictures from the <u>pier, an elevated</u>
 49

<u>wooden walkway overlooking</u> the ocean.
 49

49. A. NO CHANGE
 B. elevated pier, which serves as a walkway, overlooking
 C. pier, which is elevated and overlooks
 D. pier overlooking

For many people, the sounds of spring are

<u>associated and connected</u> with feelings of
 50

happiness and renewed vigor.

50. F. NO CHANGE
 G. coupled and associated with
 H. linked and connected
 J. associated

Problem Set 11: Redundancy

Among teenagers, apps like Snapchat and

Instagram can be <u>popular for</u> months before
51

parents find out what they are.

51. A. NO CHANGE
    B. popular and widely used
    C. really quite popular
    D. popular for the time period of

Like clockwork, the ants would <u>march, trek and</u>
52

<u>hike</u> back up the hill every summer.
52

52. F. NO CHANGE
    G. march and hike
    H. trek and march
    J. march

I always attended soccer practice after school with

<u>my coach, who taught the team how to play.</u>
53

53. A. NO CHANGE
    B. my coach, an older woman who knew how
       to play soccer.
    C. my coach, a woman we all knew.
    D. my coach.

My mother was excited when she heard about the

<u>new, state-of-the-art</u> sound system in the new car
54

models.

54. F. NO CHANGE
    G. current and recently updated
    H. what was supposed to be a new
    J. most recent

The scientist suspected that this particle

accelerator <u>may or may not offer</u> valuable
55

insights into how all of the universe works,

including at the subatomic level.

55. A. NO CHANGE
    B. might offer
    C. could indicate important
    D. might very well provide one with

Transition Words

When relating one sentence to another or one part of a sentence to another, you must choose an appropriate transition word. In order to succeed on these questions, try first taking out the transition. Then look at the two separate parts of the sentence or sentences and determine a logical relationship yourself. Once you have done this, look at the answers and see which seems to fit the relationship you determined.

Examples

Incorrect:
LeBron is the best basketball player in the world; however, he will get paid the maximum salary next year.

Correct:
LeBron is the best basketball player in the world; therefore, he will get paid the maximum salary next year.

Example Words:	**Sequence Words:**	**Contrast Words:**
To illustrate	Then	Regardless
For example	Eventually	However
For instance	Meanwhile (at the same	Yet
In fact	time)	But
Indeed	Subsequently	Still
		While
Causation Words:	**Addition Words:**	Though
Because	Likewise	Although
Since	Similarly	By contrast
Therefore	Again	On the contrary
Consequently	Additionally	Despite this
As a result	Second(ly)	In spite of this
Subsequently	Finally	Nevertheless
So		Conversely
		On the other hand
		Meanwhile
		Instead
		Even so

Problem Set 12: Transition Words

Table tennis, or ping-pong, requires a wealth of skill and accuracy. Tennis, <u>by contrast,</u> demands a
₁
great range of motion.

1. Which of the following alternatives to the underlined portion would be LEAST acceptable?
   A. though
   B. however
   C. therefore
   D. on the contrary

So, when he went to buy a new smart phone — <u>due to the unsurprising fact that</u> his old flip phone
₂
had finally broken — the salesperson tried to sell him on a waterproof model.

2. F. NO CHANGE
   G. as a result of the knowledge that
   H. although
   J. since

The salesperson was clever and, appealing to my grandfather's hobbies, described some of the applications that could be installed. <u>However, Gramps</u> could install Findmefish to locate the
₃
best fishing spots around or GolfLogix to measure the distance from his golf ball to the hole.

3. A. NO CHANGE
   B. In addition, Gramps
   C. Conversely, Gramps
   D. Gramps

The snapping turtle's shell is ideal for concealing the turtle from potential prey until the prey is too close to escape. <u>For example,</u> when a predator
₄
approaches, the turtle can hide under its shell.

4. F. NO CHANGE
   G. On the one hand,
   H. On the other hand,
   J. To illustrate,

Problem Set 12: Transition Words

Architect John A. Roebling died of tetanus before his design for the Brooklyn Bridge was completed in 1883. <u>Therefore, the</u> completed
₅
structure was the first steel-wire suspension bridge ever constructed.

5. A. NO CHANGE
   B. Though, the
   C. Meanwhile, the
   D. The

Because of this, I had not tried any new cuisine in more than six years. <u>Still,</u> I had never eaten any
₆
"exotic" foods.

6. F. NO CHANGE
   G. On the contrary,
   H. Meanwhile,
   J. In fact,

Brother Matthias was especially influential in Ruth's life <u>since</u> Ruth truly admired Matthias'
₇
strength, fairness, and calm demeanor.

7. Which of the following alternatives to the underlined portion would be LEAST acceptable?
   A. although
   B. as
   C. in that
   D. because

I was amazed by how many different tools fit on my little Swiss Army knife. I could tighten screws with my screwdriver. I could also use the saw to cut through soft woods or other soft materials. <u>Thus,</u> I could utilize the magnifying
₈
glass whenever I was having trouble seeing small details.

8. F. NO CHANGE
   G. Finally,
   H. Secondly,
   J. Nevertheless,

Problem Set 12: Transition Words

While conducting research with his brother and cooking meals for patients, Kellogg left a batch of boiled wheat out by accident. He suspected [9] that this new, flaky substance might be a hit with the patients, and he began to produce corn flakes.

9. A. NO CHANGE
   B. In addition, he suspected
   C. Nonetheless, he suspected
   D. Nevertheless, he suspected

These challenges and games were designed to build a sense of unity and cooperation. Therefore, [10] the aspect of the trip I remember most clearly is an argument I had with my best friend.

10. F. NO CHANGE
    G. For example,
    H. Nevertheless,
    J. In addition,

The United Nations peacekeeping mission is dedicated to removing all the landmines from the area. The [11] mission also attempts to stimulate economic and social development in the area.

11. A. NO CHANGE
    B. In conclusion, the
    C. In other words, the
    D. Thus, the

Natural rubber is sticky, brittle when cold, and deforms easily when warm as [12] vulcanized rubber is less sticky, more elastic, and more durable.

Nevertheless, most [13] products are made with vulcanized rubber.

12. F. NO CHANGE
    G. warm,
    H. warm, so
    J. warm, whereas

13. A. NO CHANGE
    B. Still, most
    C. Similarly, most
    D. Most

Problem Set 12: Transition Words

Though many of his films seem somewhat silly or absurd, Anderson is aware of the power of films. Well, he identifies himself with many other
₁₄
auteurs of world cinema, such as Indian director Satyajit Ray, to whom Anderson dedicated 2007's *The Darjeeling Limited.*

14. F. NO CHANGE
    G. At once,
    H. Indeed,
    J. However,

When learning to fly fish, one commonly loses control of the fly while casting. There's a rule, therefore, that all guides and participants must
₁₅
wear sunglasses at all times to protect their eyes from stray hooks.

15. A. NO CHANGE
    B. meanwhile,
    C. instead,
    D. likewise,

None of these artistic attempts were very good, but at least I could start to make out the forms I was drawing. These sketches would never make me famous, though.
₁₆

16. F. NO CHANGE
    G. nevertheless.
    H. conversely.
    J. in addition.

Olivia was persistent. Despite this, her parents
₁₇
acquiesced, allowing, even helping, her throw an after-prom party.

17. A. NO CHANGE
    B. Finally,
    C. In fact,
    D. On the other hand

Problem Set 12: Transition Words

Traditional Buddhist texts and legends chronicle

life, death, and suffering. <u>However, yoga</u> master
18

Swami Vivekananda sought to translate these

teachings into a physical regimen.

18. F. NO CHANGE
    G. Nevertheless, yoga
    H. Instead, yoga
    J. Yoga

I'm not just referring to the embarrassment of

being caught walking off with someone else's

coat. There's <u>still</u> the fact that most of my attempts
19

have been thwarting by angry townspeople or

police officers.

19. A. NO CHANGE
    B. consequently
    C. instead
    D. also

Both with the cotton gin and with interchangeable

parts, Eli Whitney applied himself to improving

an inefficient process. <u>Instead,</u> Eli Whitney made
20

a lasting impression on the world as a brilliant

inventor in two important fields.

20. F. NO CHANGE
    G. In addition,
    H. In contrast
    J. OMIT the underlined portion

<u>Although</u> fictional accounts of Americans in the
21

South are not uncommon, few records of places

like Lafayette county have survived.

21. Which of the following alternatives to the
    underlined portion would be LEAST acceptable?
    A. Whether
    B. Whereas
    C. Though
    D. While

Problem Set 12: Transition Words

It is interesting that <u>because</u> tomatoes are one
₂₂

of the most abundant foods in Europe, they

were virtually absent from 18th century cooking

because people thought they were poisonous.

22. F. NO CHANGE
    G. though
    H. since
    J. OMIT the underlined portion

Still, she wanted the puppies gone. I could have

all of them as far as she was concerned. <u>So,</u>
₂₃

<u>instead,</u> I made the leap from dog-lover to dog-
₂₃

rescuer. Online, I found the name of an animal

shelter in the region. They were willing to help me

find loving homes for these dogs. One Saturday

afternoon, we delivered all eight puppies to new

parents.

23. A. NO CHANGE
    B. (Do NOT begin new paragraph) So,
    C. (Begin new paragraph) So, after it was all
       over,
    D. (Begin new paragraph) For instance,

Modern food scientists claim that saturated fats –

found in animals – cause heart disease. <u>Similarly,</u>
₂₄

Alaskan Inuits survived mainly on whale blubber

without health issues.

24. F. NO CHANGE
    G. Therefore,
    H. Yet,
    J. So

Problem Set 12: Transition Words

There's a link between salt and high blood

pressure, and experts believe there's a connection

between high blood pressure and heart disease.

<u>Therefore,</u> there's evidence that high salt levels
  25

increase stress.

25. A. NO CHANGE
    B. Namely,
    C. On the other hand,
    D. In addition,

Coleman figured that if he opened an Irish

restaurant, <u>so</u> his fellow Irish émigrés could feel
          26

a bit more at home.

26. F. NO CHANGE
    G. than
    H. then
    J. while

The outpost gives conservationists an opportunity

to study the magnificent wolves in their natural

habitat. <u>However, scientists</u> can find the outpost
          27

by following the cairns that dot the trail.

27. A. NO CHANGE
    B. Scientists
    C. Secondly, scientists
    D. Moreover, scientists

Problem Set 12: Transition Words

Occasionally, multiple species of wolves will
28

interact while sharing the carcass of a fresh kill.

28. Which of the following alternatives to the underlined portion would NOT be acceptable?
   F. Now and then,
   G. Once in a while,
   H. Sometimes,
   J. Sparsely,

After shooting a film in Budapest for 6 months,

when Schulman relocated to Los Angeles,
29

California, with Michael Traub, a famed manger

who had seen Schulman's performances.

29. A. NO CHANGE
   B. so then
   C. after that
   D. DELETE the underlined portion

North began marketing directly to skaters rather
30

than working with the skating magazines they had
30

previously relied on.

30. F. NO CHANGE
   G. than
   H. other than
   J. rather then

One day, the store did not survive. In fact, its
31

doors were closed for six months while Wexler

raised capital and renovated.

31. A. NO CHANGE
   B. Each week,
   C. For a time,
   D. Like its predecessor,

Problem Set 12: Transition Words

The Museum of Natural History categorizes its specimens into many different categpories, all of which are quite extensive. For example, the Marine mammal section has over 30 exhibits. Visitors can see replica dolphins and live plankton samples under a microscope. <u>After all, these</u>
₃₂
<u>rooms</u> are only a small portion of the collection of biological exhibits and an even smaller portion, of the museum's total collection.

32. F. NO CHANGE
    G. These rooms, at last,
    H. Also, these rooms
    J. These rooms, however,

Mammals were long defined as warm-blooded animals that give birth to live young. The platypus, <u>similarly,</u> perplexed biologists for years
₃₃
because although it is warm-blooded, the females lay eggs.

33. A. NO CHANGE
    B. for example,
    C. additionally,
    D. however,

We sat down in the desert sands and waited for our caravan. <u>Generally,</u> a sudden gust of wind left
₃₄
us blinking as sand flew into our eyes.

34. F. NO CHANGE
    G. Furthermore,
    H. Once again,
    J. DELETE (capitalizing the A)

Problem Set 12: Transition Words

Most are there to watch a game; a few, <u>for example,</u> are likely to be music junkies there to hear a concert in the stadium.

35. A. NO CHANGE
      B. consequently,
      C. however,
      D. in fact,

In keeping with the Cathedral's elaborate style, hand-carved wooden pews embrace the stage. <u>Churchgoers</u> credit the traditional Romanesque style with adding enhancement to their experience.

36. F. NO CHANGE
      G. In the same manner, churchgoers
      H. On one hand, churchgoers
      J. For instance, churchgoers

<u>Although</u> online classes are affordable and convenient, Johnson claims that they could replace traditional schooling by 2050.

37. A. NO CHANGE
      B. Since
      C. Until
      D. Unless

Although ancient Indians and Israelites had different ingredients at their disposals, both used hot stone ovens to make flatbreads. <u>On the other hand, the</u> Indians used a special cooktop called a *tandoor*.

38. F. NO CHANGE
      G. Be that as it may, the
      H. By now, the
      J. The

Problem Set 12: Transition Words

I listened transfixed as he spoke about sheer size of our universe. I heard about far away planets and countless space features, like black holes. <u>For example, all</u> the facts and figures fascinated me. I previously had no idea how many different types of stars and asteroids existed.

39. A. NO CHANGE
    B. If so, all
    C. All
    D. In contrast, all

Though people warned me that New Yorkers were rude, everyone I <u>met, consequently,</u> was polite and helpful.

40. F. NO CHANGE
    G. met, furthermore,
    H. met, otherwise,
    J. met

The thumping of the speakers made my heart race. I began to enjoy the music, <u>for example,</u> as I danced along with the crowd.

41. A. NO CHANGE
    B. in other words,
    C. otherwise,
    D. however,

Verbs: Tense and Subject Agreement

When answer choices are verbs, you must find the subject and check the tense. Verbs are action words, or forms of the word "to be." Remember that is, are, was, and were are all verbs! The subject will always come before any prepositions (linking words such as of, by, on, around, to, etc.)
Examples: (subjects and verbs in bold, prepositions italicized):

Examples

Incorrect:
The scent *of* the roses **are** very pleasant.

Correct:
The scent *of* the roses **is** very pleasant.

Incorrect:
Had the pitcher threw the ball just a centimeter to the right, there was a good chance that the batter would be injured.

Correct:
Had the pitcher thrown the ball just a centimeter to the right, there would have been a good chance that the batter would have been injured.

Tense	Usage	Example
Present	happening now	I take the ACT
Past	completed before now	I took the ACT
Future	will happen	I will take the ACT
Present Perfect	started in the past and continues now	I have taken the ACT
Past Perfect	happened before something else in past	I had taken the ACT when I graduated.
Conditional	could happen or have happened	If I studied then I would have passed.

Problem Set 13: Verbs

The Ukrainian politician reminisced about the days before two separatist groups <u>had took</u> over
₁
parts of the Ukraine that border Russia.

1. A. NO CHANGE
   B. took
   C. taken
   D. begun to take

Last spring, I spent a semester studying abroad in Prague in the Czech Republic. At the end of the semester, I <u>had gone</u> back home to finish school
₂
in North Carolina. This year, I am applying everything I learned abroad to my studies at home.

2. F. NO CHANGE
   G. will have gone
   H. go
   J. went

Down the street from my high school, the Clucky Chicken is always open, and a friendly employee is always waiting. It <u>had been</u> on a quiet street,
₃
located between a large field and a gas station.

3. A. NO CHANGE
   B. was located
   C. was
   D. is

The thirteen stripes are red and white to honor the original thirteen colonies, and the number of stars in the corner <u>has been</u> changed over time to
₄
match the current number of states in the union.

4. F. NO CHANGE
   G. are
   H. were
   J. have been

Problem Set 13: Verbs

I could go to that store anytime, and someone

would look up from stocking shelves or cleaning

floors and <u>smiles and waves</u> at me.
       5

5.   A. NO CHANGE
      B. smiling and waving
      C. smile to wave
      D. smile and wave

With over 100,000 employees across the globe,

Microsoft has come a long way from its

inception. America's offices <u>were</u> the
            6

beneficiaries of Bill Gates' technological vision.

6.   F. NO CHANGE
      G. are
      H. had been
      J. would be

Afterwards, I went to the nearest car dealership.

Not one of the many fancy automobiles sitting in

the lot <u>were an</u> electric vehicle. Gas-guzzlers
      7

filled the dealership.

7.   A. NO CHANGE
      B. were an actual
      C. was an
      D. would have been an

Teams of Israeli soldiers are available who

<u>searches for and then destroys</u> tunnels created by
      8

Hamas.

8.   F. NO CHANGE
      G. searches for and destroy
      H. search for and destroys
      J. search for and destroy

The collective sound of dogs barking in separate

houses <u>make</u> the neighborhood seem chaotic and
      9

more stressful than it really is.

9.   A. NO CHANGE
      B. have made
      C. makes
      D. are making

Problem Set 13: Verbs

So, when he <u>went</u> to buy a new smart phone —
10

since his old flip phone had finally broken — the

salesperson tried to sell him on a waterproof

model.

10. F. NO CHANGE
    G. had went
    H. goes
    J. will go

Explaining to the confused group of ladies that he

can change the consistency of metals, <u>Blaine</u>
                                        11

<u>takes</u> a coin from an audience member and, to the
11

surprise of the crowd, seemingly bites a piece off.

11. A. NO CHANGE
    B. Blaine taking
    C. Blaine has taken
    D. Blaine took

On June 4, 1944, the weather conditions were

clearly unsuitable for a landing at Normandy.

This inclement weather <u>threatens</u> to postpone the
                         12

landing for another month.

12. F. NO CHANGE
    G. had been threatened
    H. would have threatened
    J. threatened

The committee members of our yearbook

publication <u>keeps</u> busy all year, attempting to put
             13

together the perfect yearbook for the students.

13. A. NO CHANGE
    B. are kept
    C. is kept
    D. has been kept

Problem Set 13: Verbs

Individual instruction offers guidance and insight;

gallery showings and auctions <u>reward</u> students
14

with opportunities to show and sell their work.

14. F. NO CHANGE
    G. rewarding
    H. rewarded
    J. rewards

Slowly, I learned to navigate the narrow, winding

cobblestone streets. I <u>approach them</u> as if they
15

were obstacle courses that required my full

attention.

15. A. NO CHANGE
    B. approach them,
    C. approached them
    D. approached them,

At first glance, Mawhinney's RecordRama

Archive warehouse looks like a total mess. The

many shelves <u>being overcrowded and</u> covered
16

with old vinyl records.

16. F. NO CHANGE
    G. was overcrowded and
    H. are overcrowded and
    J. overcrowded and

The Hohokam canal system is considered the

oldest and most effective pre-Columbian irrigation

system in North America. The major canals <u>have</u>
17

<u>averaged</u> between 8 and 12 miles in length. The
17

canals are tapered throughout their length to

maintain the water velocity.

17. A. NO CHANGE
    B. had averaged
    C. were
    D. are

Problem Set 13: Verbs

Medical professionals <u>have</u> been unsure how to treat bacterial infections such as Staphylococcus. In laboratory tests, Howard Florey was able to show that Fleming's penicillin effectively killed off the harmful bacteria in populations of mice.

18. F. NO CHANGE
     G. would have
     H. had
     J. will have

The boy <u>chosed</u> to play soccer instead of baseball.

19. A. NO CHANGE
     B. had chose
     C. chosen
     D. chose

Vieques is an island-municpality of Puerto Rico. The island <u>will feature</u> the largest bioluminescent bay in America and one of the most renowned in the world.

20. F. NO CHANGE
     G. features
     H. featured
     J. did feature

"Muckraker" was the term used to describe people like Tarbell who, fed up with the rampant corruption, wrote articles to expose injustice even though officials <u>threatened them</u>.

21. A. NO CHANGE
     B. threaten them
     C. threatened her
     D. threaten her

Problem Set 13: Verbs

Kafka died in 1924 without knowing that the

majority of his work <u>is</u> published posthumously,
₂₂

making him one of the most influential authors of

the 20th century.

22. F. NO CHANGE
    G. would be
    H. has been
    J. OMIT the underlined portion

The technology of computers <u>have changed</u>
₂₃

significantly since the days of MS-DOS, but

today users can still enjoy the innovations of both

Microsoft and Apple.

23. A. NO CHANGE
    B. had changed
    C. changes
    D. has changed

From the call, the producers learned that

Chappelle <u>in fact had somehow finished</u> writing
₂₄

another season and was ready to start filming.

24. F. NO CHANGE
    G. will finish
    H. would finish
    J. had finished

Perhaps this is because <u>being</u> a clown and I never
₂₅

really feel comfortable without oversized shoes.

25. A. NO CHANGE
    B. being that I'm
    C. I was
    D. I'm

For generations upon generations, this is the way

<u>things would have remained</u>. Men hunted animals
₂₆

while women gathered nuts and berries.

26. F. NO CHANGE
    G. things were to have worked.
    H. that things work.
    J. things worked.

Problem Set 13: Verbs

I'm not just referring to the embarrassment of being caught walking off with someone else's coat. There's still the fact that most of my attempts <u>have been thwarting</u> by angry townspeople or police officers.

27. A. NO CHANGE
    B. had been thwarted
    C. are thwarting
    D. are thwarted

Jeans constructed according to Levi Strauss' original instructions are so comfortable and durable that the design of his pants <u>have been</u> barely altered over time.

28. F. NO CHANGE
    G. was
    H. are
    J. were

Though Alicia Keys <u>had sang about the city's</u> "big lights," nothing could have prepared me for Times Square.

29. A. NO CHANGE
    B. has sang about the city's
    C. had sung about the city's
    D. sang about the cities

Report cards must now be mailed to students' houses. What was once posted on a bulletin board for public viewing <u>are</u> now considered private, sensitive material.

30. F. NO CHANGE
    G. is
    H. were
    J. have been

Problem Set 13: Verbs

New writers began describing race and social

class issues that <u>had previously been</u> neglected.
31

31. A. NO CHANGE
    B. have previously been
    C. are previously being
    D. are previously

Kelly Clarkson is from a small town in Texas,

where she worked at a movie theater. Fortunately,

she <u>auditions</u> for American Idol, skyrocketing her
32

to stardom.

32. F. NO CHANGE
    G. has auditioned
    H. auditioned
    J. is auditioning

At first I was scared, but the sailboat hadn't gone

far, and I realized that I <u>would of been</u> able to
33

swim ashore.

33. A. NO CHANGE
    B. would be
    C. will be
    D. should of been

Often, scientists search for explanations for what

<u>seem</u> to be unexplainable.
34

34. F. NO CHANGE
    G. seems
    H. seemed
    J. have seemed

Armstrong and Aldrin became the first astronauts

to collect moon rocks and <u>bringing</u> them back to
35

Earth to study.

35. A. NO CHANGE
    B. will bring
    C. bring
    D. is bringing

Problem Set 13: Verbs

There are two hypotheses about why Europeans used to think tomatoes were poisonous. The first offering the plant's strong resemblance to other toxic vegetables as an explanation.
36

36. F. NO CHANGE
    G. has been offered
    H. offers
    J. will offer

As the wombats ran up the hill, they were also
37
falling into single file.
37

37. A. NO CHANGE
    B. are also falling
    C. have also fallen
    D. will also fall

Many cities have began to make bikes available
38
for rent for just a few dollars per day.

38. F. NO CHANGE
    G. began
    H. beginning
    J. begun

One clear February evening when I was nine years old, I had went stargazing with my father.
39

39. A. NO CHANGE
    B. had did some
    C. gone
    D. went

"Megan, there's The Big Dipper," Dad said, he kneeled so I could spot the unmistakable
40
arrangement of stars.

40. F. NO CHANGE
    G. started to kneel
    H. kneeling
    J. and having kneeled

Problem Set 13: Verbs

These days, with authors writing up to five articles

a year, it's easy to forget that at one time writing

multiple articles a year <u>were</u> rare.

41

41. A. NO CHANGE
    B. have been
    C. was
    D. are

<u>They weren't</u> his reading skill, therefore, that

42

would impress one of the country's top professors.

42. F. NO CHANGE
    G. That wasn't
    H. They weren't
    J. It wasn't

Rather than viewing games as individual events,

seasons seem to follow a story arc. Certain story

lines <u>become</u> associated with certain teams—for

43

example, choking under pressure with the Mets.

43. A. NO CHANGE
    B. have became
    C. becomed
    D. had became

The result, in this instance and others, is language

that creates visuals and <u>told</u> a uniquely compelling

44

narrative.

44. F. NO CHANGE
    G. had told
    H. tells
    J. tell

By the end of the first year, Coleman's friends

had already doubled their money and were eager

to invest in a new location. The <u>friends will,</u>

45

however, have a lot of stress about investing even

more money.

45. A. NO CHANGE
    B. friends did,
    C. friends,
    D. friends do,

Problem Set 13: Verbs

Amazingly, tourists <u>might see</u> a grey wolf, or an
₄₆
observer could see a wolf giving birth.

46. F. NO CHANGE
    G. had saw
    H. might of seen
    J. might have saw

Traub, who planned to open a talent agency in

Los Angeles, <u>knowing</u> that there would be more
₄₇
entertainment opportunities on the west coast for

Schulman.

47. A. NO CHANGE
    B. knew
    C. and he knew
    D. known

When I was 10, I <u>have borrowed</u> a pair of roller
₄₈
skates from my friend. I never gave them back.

48. F. NO CHANGE
    G. have been borrowing
    H. were borrowed
    J. borrowed

The organic farming exhibit at the museum <u>store</u>
₄₉
all of its live animals in the Webster Center in the

Biotic Wing of the museum.

49. A. NO CHANGE
    B. has stored
    C. have stored
    D. storing

I begin my commute at 7:30 in the morning.

During my trip, other passengers <u>bumps</u> into me
₅₀
on the subway.

50. F. NO CHANGE
    G. has bumped
    H. bumped
    J. bump

Problem Set 13: Verbs

Meteorologists Kenyon and Kolber found

that tornadoes begin with the same process as

most thunderstorms and <u>forms</u> what is called a
    ₅₁

supercell.

51. A. NO CHANGE
    B. were they to form
    C. formed
    D. form

It was June and our backpacks were heavy, but we

<u>would have needed</u> gallons of water to drink as
    ₅₂

we hiked the Appalachian Trail.

52. F. NO CHANGE
    G. would need
    H. will need
    J. need

<u>Looking past</u> the houses and out towards the
    ₅₃

rolling hills made me feel powerful.

53. A. NO CHANGE
    B. Looking passed
    C. To look passed
    D. Past

During his semester in China, Lars perfected his

ability to navigate a Mandarin menu and quickly

<u>comprehend</u> street signs.
    ₅₄

54. F. NO CHANGE
    G. had been comprehending,
    H. had comprehended
    J. comprehended

Eating eggs with peanut butter <u>might of seemed to</u>
    ₅₅

<u>be</u> an odd choice.
    ₅₅

55. A. NO CHANGE
    B. could seemingly been
    C. might have seemed
    D. could seem being

Problem Set 13: Verbs

The art collector's search for the statue's sculptor

<u>led him</u> to Rome and an eventual partnership with
56

the artist.

56. F. NO CHANGE
    G. lead himself
    H. led himself
    J. lead him

Jesse's attempts to convince people he's a

teenager—whether deliberate affectations or lack

of awareness—ultimately <u>matters</u> very little, for
57

no one is ever fooled.

57. A. NO CHANGE
    B. has mattered
    C. had mattered
    D. matter

Writing Strategy

These questions always feature actual text before the answer choices are given on the right side of the page, and they are no longer actually grammar questions. Instead, they will give you goals to accomplish and ask which answer best accomplishes that goal, or they will ask you whether the author of the passage has accomplished a certain goal. Though there are a number of different writing strategy questions, they tend to fall into a few different categories that are pretty repetitive. Take a look at the guide to the different types of writing strategy questions below.

The specific goal question:

This type of question asks you as a reader which answer choice will best accomplish a very specific goal in the question. The ACT will phrase this in ways such as, "Given that all of the choices are true, which one best shows that Jonze wanted to be involved in the entertainment industry at a young age?" or "At this point the writer wants to provide a statement showing that this vacation was her personal favorite. Which choice best accomplishes this goal?" These questions tend to be straightforward: just take your time to identify the goal you must accomplish, then pick the answer that best achieves this.

The add/delete question:

This type of question asks you whether a certain phrase should either be added to or deleted from the passage. Many students find this type of question difficult, but there are two simple questions you can ask yourself to answer these correctly. First, "is the piece of information somehow related or relevant to what the author is discussing in the paragraph?" If not, then delete it. If so, then ask yourself, "is this information something that was already stated elsewhere in the passage?" If it has already been stated, delete it. If the information is new and relevant to the paragraph, keep it or insert it. Once you have decided whether to keep or delete, then look at the answer choices and decide which has the best reasoning.

The delete and lose question:

This type of question asks you what would be lost from the passage if a certain piece of text were deleted. Generally, the key to answering this type of question correctly is careful, detailed reading of the piece of text. Read the piece that is referenced by the question and then come up with your own description of what would be lost by deleting this section. Match your description with the closest answer choice.

The general goal question:

This type of question asks you which choice best accomplishes a broad goal, like transitioning from one paragraph to the next, or whether the author has completed a broad goal, like focusing on one topic throughout the essay. Make sure you pay close attention to how these questions are worded. If you are trying to give a final sentence for a paragraph, there is a large difference between a question that asks, "which of the following best concludes the preceding paragraph?" and "which of the following best leads from the preceding paragraph to the one that follows?" Similarly, be careful to note whether a question at the end of a passage asks you whether the author focused on a certain topic or merely mentioned the topic. To focus on the topic, the essay must center on that topic, but to mention the topic means it must only come up at some point in the essay.

Problem Set 14: Writing Strategy

Organic Electronics

A conductive material is one that can transmit, or conduct, an electrical charge. The vast majority of known conductive materials are inorganic materials, specifically metals, like copper or aluminum, and metal alloys, like steel and bronze. [A] When Englishman Henry Letheby discovered the first organic conductor, polyaniline, in 1862, the finding seemed insignificant compared to Letheby's work on food purity and medical applications of electricity.

<u>However, researchers in the 1960s and 1970s became intrigued by organic conductors.</u> [1] This research led to the discovery of several other organic conductive materials, and the 2000 Nobel Prize for Chemistry was awarded to Alan J. Heeger, Alan G. MacDiarmid, and Hideki Shirakawa for their joint work on polymer conductivity. [B] The first applications of organic conductivity to industry spawned from the work of Ching W. Tang, who produced the first organic

1. The writer is considering deleting the underlined sentence. Should the sentence be kept or deleted?
    A. Kept, because it indicates that research occurred between Letheby's discovery and the 2000 Nobel Prize.
    B. Kept, because it emphasizes that nobody cared about Letheby's discovery.
    C. Deleted, because it is too vague and does not mention specific researchers.
    D. Deleted, because it contradicts the point that Letheby's discovery of polyaniline seemed inisgnificant.

2019-1

Problem Set 14: Writing Strategy

diode in 1987. This breakthrough led to the emergence of the field of organic light-emitting diodes, or OLED. [C]

Currently, researchers are working on organic solar cells, which would be far cheaper to produce than our current solar cells. In order to create these organic solar cells, scientists need to purify the organic compounds.

Vacuum sublimation is the method of choice for purification of organic compounds for use in the organic electronics industry. Solid organic matter is placed in a sublimation apparatus and heated under a vacuum. <u>Bypassing the liquid phase,</u> the organic molecules transition directly from the solid to the gas phase. The gas is a purified version of the organic matter that is then cooled to create a pure solid.

2

2

As science progresses, the role of organic conductive materials continues to grow. [D] From lightbulbs to televisions and solar panels, <u>organic electronics may soon change our world.</u>

3

3

2. If the writer were to delete the underlined portion (adjusting the capitalization as needed), the sentence would primarily lose:
   F. an explanation of how organic molecules react to different pressures
   G. a visual description of the organic molecules
   H. a detail that mentions a step some organic molecules skip when transitioning from solid to gas.
   J. an explanation of how organic molecules change phases.

3. Which choice most effectively concludes the sentence and the essay?
   A. NO CHANGE
   B. most conductors will still be made of metal.
   C. organic electronics will continue to confuse scientists.
   D. organic electronics are composed of organic conductive materials.

Problem Set 14: Writing Strategy

Questions 4 and 5 ask about the preceding passage as a whole.

4. Suppose the writer's primary purpose had been to offer an example of a discovery that changed our understanding of science. Would this essay accomplish that purpose?

F. Yes, because it describes how the discovery of organic conductive materials changed how we view chemistry.

G. Yes, because it describes how the discovery of OLED changed the electronics industry.

H. No, because it focuses on how scientists are still trying to develop organic solar panels.

J. No, because it explains that organic electronics may change our lives but not our understanding of science.

5. The writer is considering adding the following sentence to the essay:

Since these diodes are thin and simple, they can be used to create flexible and even transparent displays.

If the writer were to add this sentence, it would most logically be placed at Point:

A. A in Paragraph 1

B. B in Paragraph 2

C. C in Paragraph 2

D. D in Paragraph 5

Kayaking Mosquito Bay

Wearing sweatshirts to protect ourselves

from the bugs, we watched the flickering lights of

the convenience store as we waited for our van.

[A] It was April, and the sun was setting on the
                                              6

island of Vieques, off the coast of Puerto Rico.
                                               6

I turned to my three friends and confessed: "I

don't even know what a bioluminescent bay is."

[B] As we rode down the narrow dirt path,

the old van groaned as we hit each bump, making

us doubt we would ever arrive. The path soon

changed from dirt to mud. The van slipped and

6. If the writer were to delete the preceding sentence, the paragraph would primarily lose:

F. a further explanation of the setting for the story.

G. a statement that introduces the time of year, which is the focus of the following sentence.

H. an unnecessary detail that contradicts information given earlier in the paragraph.

J. a clear image that conveys how the narrator felt as he waited.

Problem Set 14: Writing Strategy

strained but persevered until we finally reached a

clearing. [C]

After piling out of the van, we paired off

and grabbed our kayaks, setting off down the

muddy trail to Mosquito Bay. With each step, we

were bitten by a swarm of mosquitos and came to

understand the name of the bay. We finally

reached the shore and lined up behind our guides.

Once we climbed into our boats, the whole

group of kayakers—about twenty of us in all—set

off into the water in a line. Our pace slowed to

a crawl. <u>Progressing through the bay</u>, we began
                    7

to see flickers of light around our paddles. In the

dark of midnight, we began to see the entire line

of kayaks illuminate, water <u>scorching</u> beneath our
                                        8

transparent boats. We coasted through the water

and marveled at the beauty of nature.

As we paddled back to shore, I felt

inspired and amazed. I still cannot explain

the science, but I know the beauty of the

bioluminescent bay is unmatched. [D]

7. Which choice emphasizes the slowness of the
   pace and supports the idea that the narrator's
   group of friends did not set their own pace?
   A. NO CHANGE
   B. Following our guides' instructions to
      paddle cautiously,
   C. Moving along with each paddle,
   D. Proceeding through the water,

8. Which choice most dramatically emphasizes
   the brightness of the bay?
   F. NO CHANGE
   G. gleaming
   H. smothering
   J. eclipsing

Problem Set 14: Writing Strategy

| Questions 9 and 10 ask about the preceding passage as a whole. |

9. The writer wants to add the following sentence to the essay:

   > We glanced quickly at each other, grabbed our cameras, and climbed into the van with the rest of the tourists.

   The sentence would most logically be placed at Point:
   A. A in Paragraph 1
   B. B in Paragraph 2
   C. C in Paragraph 2
   D. D in Paragraph 5

10. Suppose the writer's primary purpose had been to describe an experience of doing something difficult. Would this essay accomplish that purpose?
   F. Yes, because it shows how the van struggled along the path to the bay.
   G. Yes, because it explains that the experience of walking from the van to the shore was unpleasant.
   H. No, because it states that everything about the trip was enjoyable.
   J. No, because it focuses mainly on the positive aspects of the trip and the beauty of the location.

The Art of Jean-Michel Basquiat

Born to Haitian and Puerto Rican parents in Brooklyn, the precocious child named Jean-Michel Basquiat could fluently speak, read, and write in English, Spanish, and French by age 11. However, his mother was committed to a mental institution for the first time when he was 11, and by age 17, Jean-Michel dropped out of high school and ran away from home. Though he dreamed of becoming a famous artist, Basquiat found himself sleeping on friends' couches and selling homemade T-shirts and postcards to survive.

Problem Set 14: Writing Strategy

[11] The two friends called their comic "SAMO," and one day when riding the subway back home to Brooklyn from Manhattan, Basquiat scrawled SAMO in marker for the first time. Once Basquiat dropped out of school and Diaz graduated, the two began inscribing SAMO, along with clever social commentary, on buildings all over lower Manhattan.   [12] *The Soho News* first reported on the SAMO graffiti, and Basquiat and Diaz achieved recognition when they gave up their anonymity in an article in *The Village Voice*. Basquiat and Diaz ended the SAMO graffiti project in 1979, announcing their intentions to the world by writing "SAMO is dead" on buildings all over New York. Basquiat began to focus more on his paintings, and his rise to prominence in the art world was nothing short of <u>meteoric.</u>
₁₃

   In 1980, Basquiat met Andy Warhol at a restaurant, and Warhol was so impressed with Basquiat's work that he quickly befriended the

11. Which of the following true statements would provide the best transition from the preceding paragraph to this paragraph?
A. Before dropping out of high school, Basquiat began working on a comic book with his friend Al Diaz.
B. Basquiat met Al Diaz and Shannon Dawson at the City as School high school.
C. Basquiat was friends with many artists during his time at the City as School high school.
D. Basquiat's postcards and T-shirts were not as successful as his graffiti.

12. In the preceding sentence, the clause "along with clever social commentary" primarily serves to indicate:
F. that Basquiat's political views were not yet well developed.
G. how visually striking the SAMO graffiti was to the viewer.
H. how Basquiat and Diaz's views were ahead of their time.
J. that Basquiat and Diaz included cultural critiques in their graffiti.

13. Which choice most strongly suggests that Basquiat's fame arrived quickly once he focused on his paintings?
A. NO CHANGE
B. circumstantial
C. fleeting
D. surprising

Problem Set 14: Writing Strategy

young artist. Warhol was so fond of Basquiat that he made him the subject of one of his own paintings and collaborated with him on a series of paintings between 1983 and 1985. In March 1982, Basquiat had his first solo art show at the renowned Annina Nosei gallery in SoHo; later that year he lived with famed art dealer Larry Gagosian and exhibited his work at Gagosian's gallery in West Hollywood.

[1] Basquiat's life ended far too soon, but his legacy in the world of art will endure. [2] The street art movement has only continued to grow, and street art can now be found on everything from t-shirts to presidential campaign posters. [3] Today, street artists like Banksy and Shepard Fairey carry on Basquiat's legacy. [4] He brought street art and graffiti to the forefront of the American art scene. [14]

14. For the sake of the logic and coherence of this paragraph, Sentence 4 should be placed:
    F. where it is now.
    G. before Sentence 1.
    H. after Sentence 1.
    J. after Sentence 2.

Question 15 asks about the preceding passage as a whole

---

15. Suppose the writer's primary purpose had been to write an essay summarizing the history of art in America. Would this essay accomplish that goal?
    A. Yes, because it discusses older American artists like Andy Warhol and compares them to newer artists.
    B. Yes, because it demonstrates the quality of Basquiat's street art.
    C. No, because it focuses instead on one artist and his place in the American art world.
    D. No, because it focuses instead on a history of art in New York City.

Problem Set 14: Writing Strategy

Learning to Fish Again

As far back as most of us can remember, my family has loved to take fishing trips during the summer months. Back in 1928, my great-grandfather was said to have reeled in the largest trout ever caught in Lake Michigan! Unfortunately, the increase in recreational fishing in the years since my great-grandfather lived has gradually led to serious environmental problems.

The most discussed is overfishing, which depletes fish stocks and prevents fish from reproducing. But the damage to the environment from fishing goes deeper than just overfishing. When people go fishing, they often drive – with their boats in tow – to their favorite fishing grounds. Traveling in a large camper with a boat tied behind it is not very fuel efficient and generates exhaust fumes that release harmful carbon dioxide into the atmosphere. Once they reach the fishing ground, anglers, or people who fish, launch their canoes or motorboats into the water.

Problem Set 14: Writing Strategy

Such watercraft have often been used in lakes and rivers in other parts of the state or country, and when these craft are sailed in a new body of water, small plants and animals from other places get into the lake; these "invasive species" start to reproduce, and soon they disrupt the natural balance of the lake's ecosystem. When these species <u>migrate</u> into the lake, the lake's
¹⁶
original residents get pushed out.

Recently, my family has joined a new angler's group active here around Lake Michigan that is dedicated to making sure recreational anglers use responsible practices when they go fishing. Instead of driving with our motorboat to a <u>nearby</u> fishing-ground, we rent a boat when we
¹⁷
get to our chosen spot. On shore, we buy only live bait lures that are native to the lake. We then climb into the boat and set sail. Even with these extra precautions, fishing with my family still feels casual and relaxed.

16. Which choice best characterizes the preceding sentence's description of the process by which invasive species get into the lake from other places?
   F. NO CHANGE
   G. Hitchhike
   H. Move themselves
   J. Swim

17. If the writer were to delete the underlined portion, the sentence would primarily lose:
   A. an allusion to where the writer takes vacations.
   B. a clarification that the writer is primarily discussing fishing-grounds.
   C. a suggestion that the writer lives near Lake Michigan.
   D. an indication that the writer prefers fishing in Lake Michigan to fishing in other places.

Problem Set 14: Writing Strategy

The summer sun beams down on me, my brothers, and my parents. All day long we catch smallmouth bass, lake trout, and yellow perch. Seeing these native species thriving in their natural habitat makes me proud to be doing my part to protect the unique ecosystem of this beautiful lake. And the best part is yet to come – fresh lake trout for dinner!

Question 18 asks about the preceding passage as a whole

18. Suppose the writer's goal had been to write an essay focusing on the ecological impact of invasive species on fragile ecosystems. Would this essay accomplish that goal?
    F. Yes, because the essay describes the author's concern about invasive species and the steps he took to address those concerns.
    G. Yes, because the essay offers a scientific explanation of the damage done by invasive species.
    H. No, because the essay primarily focuses on the author's own experiences.
    J. No, because they essay states that overfishing is a more serious problem than invasive species.

Giacomo Puccini: A Life in Opera

Giacomo Puccini, one of the most popular composers in history, wrote numerous pieces of music, including some of the world's most beloved operas – pieces which are often performed today. <u>Born in Italy in 1858, Puccini began his career singing as a boy soprano and playing as a substitute organist in the church where his father worked.</u>
19

19. Given that all the choices are true, which one ends the paragraph with the strongest indication that Puccini was active as a musician from an early age?
    A. NO CHANGE
    B. gained a worldwide fame that brought him to many different countries during his long and productive career.
    C. lived much of life in Milan, the city where he first developed his signature style that combines musical complexity with a child-like simplicity.
    D. was deeply committed to the education of young musicians and composers throughout his life.

Problem Set 14: Writing Strategy

Many of Puccini's most popular operas have stories that take place in foreign lands. Japan, The United States, and France are only some of the countries that are used as settings for his works. For example, *Madame Butterfly* tells the story of a young Japanese girl who is abandoned by her American husband. <u>Heavy stuff,</u>[20] <u>but that's what opera is all about, right</u>[20]? In *La Boheme,* Puccini tells the story of a young poet, Rudolfo, and his <u>beautiful</u>[21] girlfriend, Mimi. Their relationship ultimately ends when Mimi becomes so sick from tuberculosis that she dies.

[1] *Il Trittico*, one of Puccini's later compositions, is a trilogy consisting of three short operas that are meant to be performed together. [2] Each opera is written in one particular genre. [3] The complete trilogy – a horror story, a tragedy, and a comedy – invites listeners to experience the many strong emotions popular in opera. [4] Though Puccini's operas deal at times with morose subject matter – be it illness,

20. F. NO CHANGE
    G. Crazy, no?
    H. Could it be?
    J. DELETE the underlined portion.

21. Given that all the choices accurately reflect the story in Puccini's opera, which one most clearly suggests what it is about the girlfriend that results in her fate?
    A. NO CHANGE
    B. Ailing
    C. New
    D. Beloved

abandonment in love, or poverty – each one is

filled with characters who are charming,

interesting, and wonderfully alive. [5] The

combination of dark subject matter and

sympathetic characters is perhaps most evident in

his 1900 opera *Tosca*. [6] Here, in a two-act work

filled with dramatic action, Puccini allows for a

good deal of violence and death. [7] However,

the characters, including the heroine Tosca, her

lover Cavaradossi, and the villain Scarpia, are

all fascinating and beautifully human. [8] The

same could be said of Puccini himself. [9] He led

an eventful life filled with success, failure, and

scandal – but how different is that from many of

the celebrities we know and love today? 22

22. The writer wants to divide this paragraph into two so that the first paragraph focuses exclusively on Puccini's operatic trilogy. The best place to begin the new paragraph would be at the beginning of Sentence:
    F. 4
    G. 5
    H. 6
    J. 7

Question 23 asks about the preceding passage as a whole

---

23. Suppose the writer's goal had been to write an essay about a composer with a long and successful career. Would this essay have accomplished that goal?
    A. Yes, because it focuses on a composer and states that his most important compositions are based on his musical education as a child.
    B. Yes, because it focuses on a composer who wrote music for many years and wrote many compositions, quite a few of which are still popular now.
    C. No, because even though it focuses on a successful composer, it does not provide the exact composition dates for each of his operas.
    D. No, because it focuses on what inspired a particular composer but does not indicate whether he was successful.

Problem Set 14: Writing Strategy

Julia Child: The Chef Who Loved France

The American chef Julia Child (1912-2004) loved the cuisine of France. From the 1960s through the 1980s, she wrote books and appeared on television shows where she celebrated the deliciousness and variety of French cuisine ranging from fine cheeses to herbs to sauces for beef and chicken. 24

Child appreciated not only the special ingredients used in French cooking but also the careful way that French meals are prepared. She once said, "In France, cooking is a serious art form and a national sport." In her book Mastering the *Art of French Cooking, Volume 1* (1961), Child begins with a detailed list of pots, pans, graters, and other cooking tools that would be common in a typical French kitchen. The tools that a French chef would use are just as important as the ingredients themselves. This list of tools is followed by detailed descriptions of specific cooking techniques, like poaching, pureeing, and

24. If the writer were to delete the phrase "ranging from fine cheeses to herbs to sauces for beef and chicken" (placing a period after the word cuisine), the paragraph would primarily lose:
    F. a sense of the variety of French ingredients that intrigued Child.
    G. a hint at why Child preferred French cuisine to American cuisine.
    H. an explanation of why Child appreciated French cooking.
    J. several examples of specific dishes that Child enjoyed preparing.

Problem Set 14: Writing Strategy

sautéing.

In Mastering the Art of French Cooking, Volume 2 (1970), Child expands upon the cooking techniques introduced in the first volume by including baking and charcuterie. These more advanced cooking styles are explained using carefully written instructions as well as clear illustrations. 25

The culinary culture of France was also essential to Child's popular TV cooking show, *The French Chef.* On the show, Child created recipes that emphasized fresh and, at the time, unusual ingredients. When the show first ran from 1963 to 1973, French food was thought of as expensive and not suitable for home cooking. Child showed that this was not true, and her cheerful and down-to-earth manner as she cooked soufflés and other French specialities convinced home chefs in America that they could do it too. Child showed regular Americans that the delights of French cooking were within their reach.

25. Which of the following true statements, if added here, would draw a conclusion most consistent with the information presented in this paragraph?
   A. Desserts were another type of food that Child loved to cook.
   B. Child's favorite baked goods were croissants and eclairs.
   C. Child also starred in a popular television cooking show.
   D. The addition of these two styles gave chefs who already had Volume 1 a more complete understanding of French cuisine.

Problem Set 14: Writing Strategy

Shortly before she died at the age of ninety-two, Child completed an autobiography titled *My Life in France*. In it, she writes about her time in France with her husband in the years after World War II. Child includes the story of <u>how her</u> <u>husband came to work in France as an American</u> <u>diplomat.</u>
26
26
26

26. Given that all the choices are true, which one is most consistent with the main focus of the essay?
   F. NO CHANGE
   G. how she met her husband through her work for the government during the war.
   H. how her successful cookbook was transformed into an iconic television show.
   J. how she first fell in love with French food when she was served a delightful seafood dish on the day she arrived in Paris.

> Question 27 asks about the preceding passage as a whole

27. Suppose the writer were interested in conveying a source of Child's inspiration as a chef. Would the essay successfully fulfill the writer's goal?
   A. Yes, because the essay describes the central role of French cuisine in Child's career.
   B. Yes, because the essay details how Child's experiences during World War II inspired her to become a chef.
   C. No, because the essay only gives two examples of Child's cookbooks.
   D. No, because the essay does not identify Child's favorite dish to prepare.

Problem Set 14: Writing Strategy

Cesar Chavez - Labor Activist

The son of Mexican-American laborers, Cesar Estrada Chavez understood the challenges facing itinerant Latino farm workers, making him a powerful champion in their fight for rights in the mid-twentieth century. After his family lost their ranch and store during the Great Depression, Chavez, his parents, and his four siblings moved to California in the 1930s in an attempt to start again. There, to support themselves, the whole family began working as day laborers on fruit and nut farms. Chavez experienced first-hand the difficulties that plagued Latino farm workers, such as low wages and exposure to toxic pesticides. [28]

The conditions prompted Chavez to become politically active. In 1952, he became an organizer for the Community Service Organization (CSO), a Latino advocacy group. While working for the CSO, Chavez traveled throughout California, making speeches in

28. If the writer were to delete the preceding sentence, the paragraph would primarily lose a statement that:
   F. explains how farm owners attempted to alleviate the workplace burdens laborers faced in the 1930s.
   G. offers examples of issues that fueled laborers' desire for reform in the 1930s.
   H. describes the workplace reforms that prompted the Chavez family to become farm workers.
   J. evaluates attitudes toward farming that were prevalent at the time.

support of workers' rights. He was highly

effective in spreading the message of the CSO

and in attracting new followers. By 1958,

Chavez had become the CSO's national director.

Later, in 1962, he co-founded an important labor

union, the United Farm Workers (UFW). An

expert communicator, Chavez drew attention to

exploitation and injustice by organizing highly

visible acts of civil disobedience, like strikes

and boycotts. He criticized farm owners and

agricultural businesses that, he believed, created

disadvantages for farm workers by ignoring their

rights to reasonable payment and safe working

conditions. Chavez spread his message through

speeches and hunger strikes, which called

attention to people and organizations that he

felt were promoting injustice. Chavez faced his

opposition fearlessly and presented his point of

view as the morally correct one. His speeches are

known for their clear, plain language and deep

sense of moral fairness.

Problem Set 14: Writing Strategy

For example, he once said <u>"There is</u>²⁹

<u>no such thing as defeat in non-violence."</u> Such²⁹

uncompromising moral ideas formed the core

of Cesar Chavez's thinking and work. In the

early 1970s, Chavez's leadership resulted in one

of the most important labor actions in United

States history, the so-called "Salad Bowl strikes"

organized by the UFW. <u>In 1986, Chavez became</u>³⁰

<u>an important advisor to the revised Federal</u>³⁰

<u>Immigration Act.</u>³⁰

29. Which of the following accurate quotations would be best to conclude the paragraph and create an effective transition into the next sentence?
   A. NO CHANGE
   B. "You cannot uneducate the person who has learned to read."
   C. "The people who give you their food give you their hearts."
   D. "Once you help people, most become loyal."

30. Given that all the choices are true, which one most effectively concludes the paragraph and the essay by maintaining the essay's focus on the effectiveness of Chavez's political activism on behalf of farm workers?
   F. NO CHANGE
   G. Although the UFW's power ultimately weakened, other labor unions have used its tactics and recruitment techniques.
   H. After the "Salad Bowl strikes," Chavez turned his attention to organizing Filipino-American farm workers.
   J. In the 1980s, Chavez's ability to organize people and publicize issues led to significant reforms in the use of toxic pesticides that were harming workers.

> Question 31 asks about the preceding
> passage as a whole

31. Suppose the writer's goal had been to write an informative essay tracing the broad changes in a labor union's goals. Does this essay accomplish that goal?
   A. Yes, because the essay clearly explains how the UFW was created and describes the development of its platform.
   B. Yes, because the essay explains how Chavez altered the mission of the UFW over the course of several years.
   C. No, because the essay focuses on Chavez's involvement with the UFW, not on changes within the union itself.
   D. No, because the essay fails to establish the UFW as an important union.

Problem Set 14: Writing Strategy

During the potatoes famine, Sean Coleman, was among the <u>series of</u> Irish immigrants in New York
₃₂
City who were building the subway.

32. Which choice most strongly emphasizes that building the subway was widespread among Irish immigrants in New York?
   F. NO CHANGE
   G. numbered
   H. cast of
   J. countless

By her early twenties, Sheila Slate had already completed <u>a fair number of Ironman races.</u>
₃₃

33. Which choice provides the most specific indication of Slate's early achievement?
   A. NO CHANGE
   B. races.
   C. multiple Ironman races.
   D. over twenty Ironman races.

<u>When I called,</u> Grandma wanted to know if I had
₃₄
been hurt in the car accident, I assured her it was

just a fender-bender.

34. Given that all the choices are true, which one most strongly reinforces that the narrator's grandmother is anxious about the narrator's health?
   F. NO CHANGE
   G. As soon as I called,
   H. Having given the matter some thought,
   J. After hearing from me,

Chester made a delicious Thanksgiving feast for

30 despite the fact that his culinary skills were, <u>as</u>
₃₅

<u>he put it,</u> "slender."
₃₅

35. The writer is considering deleting the underlined portion (adjusting the punctuation as needed). Should the underlined portion be kept or deleted?
   A. Kept, because it serves as the only indication that it was Chester himself who described his culinary skills as lacking.
   B. Kept, because it emphasizes how unqualified Chester was to make a Thanksgiving feast for 30.
   C. Deleted, because it presents Chester in an unflattering light.
   D. Deleted, because it weakens the point that Chester performed an extraordinary feat.

Problem Set 14: Writing Strategy

In 1519, Ferdinand Magellan, <u>a page to Queen</u>
₃₆

<u>Lenor in the Portuguese Royal Court,</u> was
₃₆

selected by King Charles I of Spain to search for a

westward route to the Maluku Islands.

36. If the writer were to delete the underlined portion (adjusting the punctuation as needed), the sentence would primarily lose:
   F. a comment that discusses the various professions Magellan held.
   G. a detail that, in part, explains Magellan's connection to royalty.
   H. a claim about Magellan that shifts the focus of the paragraph away from Queen Lenor.
   J. an aside that introduces the two men who are the main focus of the essay.

(37) My teacher told me if I talked one more time

in class I would have to "scrub every inch of the

classroom" with a toothbrush until every surface

was "so shiny you could see your reflection in it."

37. The use of quotation marks around two phrases in this preceding sentence is most likely intended to:
   A. suggest that the task of cleaning the room would be one the narrator would have to struggle to accomplish
   B. distinguish the teacher's exact words from the essay writer's paraphrase of the directive
   C. emphasize that the teacher did not really mean what she said.
   D. add drama and flair to an otherwise plain narrative.

In the late 1700s, America was a brand new nation

with many different regions and cultures, <u>even</u>
₃₈

<u>different currencies in each states.</u>
₃₈

38. Given that all of the choices are true, which choice best emphasizes the presence of "different regions and cultures"?
   F. NO CHANGE
   G. and many British loyalists returned to Britain after the war.
   H. but Southern cooking would not be recognized until the 19th century.
   J. which is often true of newly formed countries.

Problem Set 14: Writing Strategy

<u>By bypassing the liquid phase,</u> dry ice sublimates
³⁹

directly into carbon dioxide gas.

39. If the writer were to delete the underlined portion (adjusting the capitalization as needed) the sentence would primarily lose:
    A. an explanation of the process carbon dioxide undergoes to change from liquid to vapor to solid.
    B. a detail that mentions a step some carbon dioxide molecules skip in changing from solid to vapor.
    C. a visual description of what carbon dioxide molecules look like
    D. an explanation of how carbon dioxide molecules react to various air temperatures.

Goat species that travel extensively have thick

wool that protects the goat <u>at times like these.</u>
⁴⁰

40. Given that all of the choices are true, which one provides the most specific information about the goat's behavior?
    F. NO CHANGE
    G. from freezing while trekking long distances over glaciers.
    H. as it performs the functions for which it is so well adapted.
    J. from external matter that might pose a problem for the goat.

Before standardized measurements, people made

makeshift units, <u>which were often very inaccurate.</u>
⁴¹

41. Given that all of the choices are true, which one most specifically describes what was sometimes used to make measurements?
    A. NO CHANGE
    B. such as containers that had other household uses.
    C. often using hands and feet as lengths and pinches and spoons as volumes.
    D. making do with whatever they could find around the house.

Problem Set 14: Writing Strategy

One boxer, Bob "The Bear" Schulman, a young

Jewish man from the Bronx, <u>was a popular boxer.</u>
                                    42

After shooting a film in Budapest for 6 months,

Schulman relocated to Los Angeles, California,

with Michael Traub, a famed manager who <u>had</u>
                                          43

<u>seen Schulman's performances.</u>
        43

42. Given that all choices are true, which one makes clear that Schulman was unmatched in his ability to attract spectators to a boxing match in which he was participating?
    F. NO CHANGE
    G. would awe spectators with his enigmatic fighting style.
    H. was a participant in many of the major fights.
    J. drew more fans to a fight than did any other fighter.

43. Given that all the choices are true, which one most clearly and effectively establishes the personal and business relationship between Schulman and Traub?
    A. NO CHANGE
    B. believed Schulman was talented.
    C. had worked in the entertainment industry for decades.
    D. had become Schulman's close friend and career manager.

Problem Set 15: Word Choice/Vocab

Over the years, I have <u>gained</u> notoriety among my

family and friends as a wonderful chef.

1. Which of the following alternatives to the underlined portion would NOT be acceptable?
   - A. developed
   - B. earned
   - C. promoted
   - D. acquired

Little is known about my great-grandfatther <u>accept</u>

that he worked as a dairy farmer and later as a ma-

gician's assistant.

2.
   - F. NO CHANGE
   - G. except that
   - H. except for
   - J. accepting

During what could be <u>summarized</u> an

apprenticeship, Plato studied law, astronomy,

mathematics and philosophy at the famous

Socratic school.

3.
   - A. NO CHANGE
   - B. called
   - C. exclaimed
   - D. cited

The use of solar panels to power homes would

<u>discharge</u> huge environmental benefits through

reduced carbon emissions.

4.
   - F. NO CHANGE
   - G. yield
   - H. relinquish
   - J. emit

So far, computer programming has rarely been

taught in high schools <u>isolating</u> specialized cases

like math and science magnet programs.

5.
   - A. NO CHANGE
   - B. the exception to which is a use in
   - C. exempting
   - D. except in

Problem Set 15: Word Choice/Vocab

She learned that the Swahili language was a

<u>fusion</u> of Arabic, German, Portuguese, English,
6

French and a few Indian languages.

6. Which of the following alternatives to the underlined portion is LEAST acceptable?
   F. grouping
   G. combination
   H. blend
   J. mixture

Throughout his travels, Lars would meticulously

describe, in writing and through pictures, each

exotic fruit he tried, including details about how it

tasted, smelled, <u>seemed, and handled</u>.
7

7. A. NO CHANGE
   B. appeared, and touched.
   C. looked, and felt.
   D. saw, and sensed.

Marines live together in barracks with bunks, a

shower and toilet, a television, and <u>an array</u> of
8

movies to watch.

8. Which of the following alternatives to the underlined portion would be LEAST acceptable?
   F. a supply
   G. a collection
   H. an assortment
   J. a classification

How disappointed early photographers would be

to see this public <u>display</u> of selfies.
9

9. Which of the following alternatives to the underlined portion would be LEAST acceptable?
   A. exhibition
   B. attraction
   C. spectacle
   D. showing

Problem Set 15: Word Choice/Vocab

The art collector's search for the statue's sculptor

led him to Rome and <u>an eventual</u> partnership with
10

the artist.

10. Which choice most strongly suggests that the artist's partnership with the art collector was not formed right away upon the art collector's arrival in Rome?
    F. NO CHANGE
    G. A circumstantial
    H. a momentary
    J. a timely

A sudden gap in the clouds blinded us as the

sunlight <u>squelched out</u> the harsh landscape of
11

jagged rock.

11. Which choice most dramatically emphasizes the ruggedness of the landscape?
    A. NO CHANGE
    B. shattered over
    C. smothered
    D. went over

Answer Keys

Problem Set 1: Adjectives and Adverbs

1. B	6. F	11. C
2. H	7. C	12. F
3. A	8. J	
4. H	9. B	
5. D	10. J	

Problem Set 2: Clarity

1. C	16. F	31. D	46. F
2. G	17. C	32. J	47. J
3. D	18. H	33. C	48. H
4. H	19. C	34. G	49. B
5. D	20. G	35. C	
6. J	21. B	36. J	
7. C	22. F	37. D	
8. F	23. D	38. H	
9. D	24. F	39. C	
10. H	25. C	40. J	
11. B	26. H	41. B	
12. J	27. B	42. A	
13. B	28. F	43. B	
14. F	29. B	44. G	
15. A	30. J	45. D	

Problem Set 3: Comparative and Superlative

1. C	6. F	11. B
2. F	7. D	12. F
3. C	8. J	
4. G	9. B	
5. D	10. F	

Problem Set 4: Idioms

1. A	11. A	21. A	31. D
2. H	12. H	22. H	32. J
3. C	13. A	23. D	
4. F	14. F	24. G	
5. D	15. A	25. C	
6. F	16. H	26. J	
7. B	17. D	27. C	
8. J	18. J	28. J	
9. D	19. B	29. C	
10. F	20. F	30. F	

Problem Set 5: Misplaced Modification

1. A	6. J	11. D	16. H	21. D
2. J	7. C	12. G	17. C	22. F
3. D	8. G	13. C	18. G	23. B
4. G	9. B	14. G	19. B	
5. B	10. F	15. A	20. J	

Problem Set 6: Noun/Pronoun Agreement

1. B	6. F	11. D	16. H	21. D
2. F	7. C	12. F	17. D	22. G
3. B	8. J	13. B	18. F	23. B
4. H	9. D	14. J	19. A	24. F
5. B	10. G	15. A	20. H	

Problem Set 7: Organization

1. D	6. F
2. F	7. A
3. B	8. F
4. J	9. C
5. B	10. J

Problem Set 8: Parallelism

1. C	6. H	11. A
2. F	7. D	12. G
3. B	8. H	13. C
4. F	9. B	14. F
5. D	10. H	

Problem Set 9: Possessives

1. B	11. B	21. C	31. A	41. B
2. G	12. F	22. F	32. F	
3. D	13. D	23. C	33. B	
4. H	14. J	24. J	34. H	
5. D	15. B	25. A	35. C	
6. J	16. F	26. G	36. J	
7. A	17. C	27. A	37. C	
8. J	18. G	28. F	38. H	
9. B	19. C	29. D	39. B	
10. G	20. J	30. G	40. G	

Answer Keys

Problem Set 10: Punctuation

1. C	31. A	61. A	91. A	121. D
2. J	32. G	62. H	92. J	122. F
3. D	33. D	63. C	93. C	123. A
4. G	34. G	64. G	94. J	124. J
5. B	35. C	65. C	95. D	125. B
6. J	36. F	66. H	96. F	126. J
7. D	37. B	67. C	97. A	127. A
8. F	38. F	68. H	98. H	128. J
9. C	39. A	69. D	99. B	129. A
10. J	40. H	70. J	100. H	130. H
11. A	41. B	71. A	101. C	131. B
12. G	42. J	72. H	102. F	132. H
13. A	43. D	73. C	103. B	133. B
14. H	44. F	74. H	104. H	134. F
15. B	45. D	75. B	105. C	135. B
16. F	46. G	76. H	106. F	136. F
17. D	47. D	77. D	107. D	137. B
18. H	48. H	78. H	108. F	138. F
19. A	49. B	79. C	109. D	139. C
20. G	50. J	80. H	110. G	140. G
21. C	51. A	81. C	111. B	141. B
22. F	52. H	82. H	112. F	142. H
23. A	53. C	83. A	113. C	143. A
24. F	54. F	84. F	114. H	144. H
25. A	55. D	85. C	115. B	145. A
26. J	56. G	86. H	116. H	
27. B	57. B	87. D	117. B	
28. H	58. J	88. G	118. G	
29. D	59. C	89. A	119. A	
30. J	60. F	90. G	120. J	

Problem Set 11: Redundancy

1. C	11. A	21. D	31. A	41. D	51. A
2. F	12. F	22. J	32. H	42. J	52. J
3. D	13. C	23. D	33. D	43. D	53. D
4. G	14. J	24. F	34. H	44. J	54. J
5. D	15. D	25. D	35. B	45. D	55. B
6. J	16. J	26. F	36. J	46. J	
7. B	17. D	27. D	37. C	47. A	
8. H	18. F	28. J	38. G	48. J	
9. D	19. B	29. A	39. D	49. D	
10. G	20. F	30. G	40. J	50. J	

Problem Set 12: Transition Words

1. C	11. A	21. A	31. D	41. D
2. J	12. J	22. G	32. J	
3. D	13. D	23. B	33. D	
4. H	14. H	24. H	34. J	
5. D	15. A	25. A	35. C	
6. J	16. F	26. H	36. F	
7. A	17. B	27. B	37. B	
8. G	18. J	28. J	38. J	
9. A	19. D	29. D	39. C	
10. H	20. J	30. F	40. J	

Problem Set 13: Verbs

1. B	16. H	31. A	46. F
2. J	17. D	32. H	47. B
3. D	18. H	33. B	48. J
4. F	19. D	34. G	49. B
5. D	20. G	35. C	50. J
6. G	21. A	36. H	51. D
7. C	22. G	37. A	52. G
8. J	23. D	38. G	53. A
9. C	24. J	39. D	54. F
10. F	25. D	40. H	55. C
11. A	26. J	41. C	56. F
12. J	27. B	42. J	57. D
13. B	28. G	43. A	
14. F	29. C	44. H	
15. C	30. G	45. B	

Problem Set 14: Writing Strategy

1. A	11. A	21. B	31. C	41. C
2. H	12. J	22. F	32. J	42. J
3. A	13. A	23. B	33. D	43. D
4. J	14. H	24. F	34. G	
5. C	15. C	25. D	35. A	
6. F	16. G	26. J	36. G	
7. B	17. C	27. A	37. B	
8. G	18. H	28. G	38. F	
9. B	19. A	29. A	39. B	
10. J	20. J	30. J	40. G	

Answer Keys

Problem Set 15: Word Choice/Vocab

1. C	6. F	11. B
2. G	7. C	
3. B	8. J	
4. G	9. B	
5. D	10. F	

ACT Essay Strategy

The ACT essay will now give you 40 minutes to read the given prompt and respond with a coherent, organized essay. While the essay will be scored on the familiar 1-36 scale, the score will not actually count toward your composite score, though schools can see your essay separately. The text at the top of the page will give you the basic topic of the prompt. In the middle of the page, you will find three possible perspectives on the topic. At the bottom of the page, you will find the actual essay prompt and assignment. You may agree or disagree with the prompts given, but you must clearly state your position and address the other positions given. Your response should follow the basic outline below.

General Statement

Thesis

Thesis

General Statement

If you'd like some practice writing the essay, go ahead and try writing some using our practice prompts on the following pages.

Challenging Authority

Is it sometimes necessary to challenge what people in authority claim to be true? We know that some respect for authority is, no doubt, necessary in order for any group or organization to function, but does questioning the people in charge - even if they are experts or leaders in their fields - make us better thinkers? Does questioning authority force all concerned to defend old ideas and decisions and to consider new ones?

Read and carefully consider these perspectives. Each suggests a particular way of thinking about challenging authority.

Perspective One	Perspective Two	Perspective Three
Not everyone is or should be entitled to an opinion. By paying too much attention to non-experts, who always numerically outweigh experts, we risk losing important insight by missing information in a sea of uninformed opinions.	The only constant in life is change. As such, it is our duty as citizens and individuals to consistently challenge authority. Each generation has the ability to find answers for problems that are particular to their time and culture.	Once a decision has been made, it is almost always best for those who are not in charge to go along with what has been decided. Even if the decision is not the ideal course of action it is better not to challenge authority, for it is better to be unified behind a subpar plan than to have no plan at all.

Essay Task

Write a unified, coherent essay in which you evaluate multiple perspectives on whether it is important to question the ideas and decisions of people in positions of authority. In your essay, be sure to:

- analyze and evaluate the perspectives given

- state and develop your own perspective on the issue

- explain the relationship between your perspective and those given

Your perspective may be in full agreement with any of the others, in partial agreement, or wholly different. Whatever the case, support your ideas with logical reasoning and detailed, persuasive examples.

Fixing Our Communities

Many people believe that our government should do more to solve our problems. After all, how can one individual create more jobs or make more roads safer or improve the schools or help to provide any of the benefits that we have come to enjoy? And yet expecting that the government- rather than individuals- should always come up with solutions to society's ills may have made us less self-reliant, undermining our independence and self-sufficiency. Should people take more responsibility for solving problems that affect their communities or the nation in general?

Read and carefully consider these perspectives. Each suggests a particular way of thinking about government's role in improving communities.

Perspective One	Perspective Two	Perspective Three
People only care about themselves and their individual property. Therefore, it is essential that the government take control in guiding improvements to communities as a whole.	No one knows the community quite like a normal community member. People are generally invested in their communities, and their intimate knowledge of what needs fixing makes them the best agents for change in a community.	Improving things takes resources. Time and money are not easy to come by. Only a large central government can effectively use these resources to make positive changes.

Essay Task

Write a unified, coherent essay in which you evaluate multiple perspectives on whether the government should have a direct role in improving communities. In your essay, be sure to:

- analyze and evaluate the perspectives given

- state and develop your own perspective on the issue

- explain the relationship between your perspective and those given

Your perspective may be in full agreement with any of the others, in partial agreement, or wholly different. Whatever the case, support your ideas with logical reasoning and detailed, persuasive examples.

Using Knowledge

Knowledge is power. In agriculture, medicine, and industry, for example, knowledge has liberated us from hunger, disease, and tedious labor. Today, however, our knowledge has become so powerful that it is out of our control. We know how to do many things, but we do not know where, when, or even whether this know-how should be used. Can knowledge be a burden rather than a benefit?

Read and carefully consider these perspectives. Each suggests a particular way of thinking about the role of human knowledge.

Perspective One	Perspective Two	Perspective Three
Progress is good and essentially linear. Whatever problems we encounter today will be solved by discoveries tomorrow.	While we may possess much technical knowledge, our knowledge about the larger questions in life is more limited than ever. As a society we are not good at talking about our deepest beliefs and emotions.	When knowledge is put to use, we often tamper with the natural order of things. Sometimes life is more harmonious when we lack knowledge.

Essay Task

Write a unified, coherent essay in which you evaluate multiple perspectives on whether knowledge is a burden or a benefit. In your essay, be sure to:

- analyze and evaluate the perspectives given

- state and develop your own perspective on the issue

- explain the relationship between your perspective and those given

Your perspective may be in full agreement with any of the others, in partial agreement, or wholly different. Whatever the case, support your ideas with logical reasoning and detailed, persuasive examples.

The Pace of Life

Technology promises to make our lives easier, freeing up time for leisure pursuits. But the rapid pace of technological innovation and the split second processing capabilities of computers that can work virtually nonstop have made us all feel rushed. We have adopted the relentless pace of the very machines that were supposed to simplify our lives, with the result that, whether at work or play, people do not feel like their lives have changed for the better. This all begs the question, do changes that make our lives easier not necessarily make them better?

Read and carefully consider these perspectives. Each suggests a particular way of thinking about the role of convenience and ease in our daily lives.

Perspective One	Perspective Two	Perspective Three
When technology makes aspects of life and business easier, we often begin to devalue the pleasures of completing simple tasks. Sometimes completing a craft by hand can be more fulfilling than doing so easily with a machine.	Technology not only makes work easier but also makes leisure easier. Our access to entertainment has never been easier, and as a result, more fulfilling.	There is always more work to be done. The addition of technology that makes work easier simply means that we, as workers, are expected to get more done in a day. This actually adds stress to our daily lives.

Essay Task

Write a unified, coherent essay in which you evaluate multiple perspectives on whether changes that make our lives easier necessarily make them better. In your essay, be sure to:

- analyze and evaluate the perspectives given

- state and develop your own perspective on the issue

- explain the relationship between your perspective and those given

Your perspective may be in full agreement with any of the others, in partial agreement, or wholly different. Whatever the case, support your ideas with logical reasoning and detailed, persuasive examples.

The Power of Conscience

A mistakenly cynical view of human behavior holds that people are primarily driven by selfish motives: the desire for wealth, for power, or for fame. Yet history gives us many examples of individuals who have sacrificed their own welfare for a cause or a principle that they regard as more important than their own lives. Conscience- that powerful inner voice that tells us what is right and what is wrong- can be a more compelling force than money, power, or fame. Is conscience a more powerful motivator than money, fame, or power?

Read and carefully consider these perspectives. Each suggests a particular way of thinking about the role of conscience in decision-making.

Perspective One	Perspective Two	Perspective Three
When people are pushed to their limits, more often than not they put self-interest first. As organisms, we have a desire to achieve certain things and protect ourselves regardless of how that affects others.	Our conscience is part of what makes us uniquely human and, as a result, is supremely powerful.	The importance of conscience is situational and both culture and circumstance influence how strongly the idea of conscience influences our actions.

Essay Task

Write a unified, coherent essay in which you evaluate multiple perspectives on whether conscience is a more powerful motivator than money, power, or fame. In your essay, be sure to:

- analyze and evaluate the perspectives given

- state and develop your own perspective on the issue

- explain the relationship between your perspective and those given

Your perspective may be in full agreement with any of the others, in partial agreement, or wholly different. Whatever the case, support your ideas with logical reasoning and detailed, persuasive examples.

Be Careful What You Wish For

The old saying "be careful what you wish for" may be an appropriate warning. The drive to achieve a particular goal can dangerously narrow one's perspective and encourage the fantasy that success in one endeavor will solve all of life's difficulties. In fact, success can sometimes have unexpected consequences. Those who propel themselves toward the achievement of one goal often find that their lives are worse once "success" is achieved than they were before. In short, can success be disastrous?

Read and carefully consider these perspectives. Each suggests a particular way of thinking about how we view the phenomenon of success.

Perspective One	Perspective Two	Perspective Three
By single mindedly pursuing success in a narrow field, we will surely miss out on other parts of life. The key to a fulfilled life is not success, but rather a balance of priorities.	The only lasting contributions to society that we remember are the product of the intense focus that creates success. There would be no Mona Lisa, Golden Gate Bridge, iPhones, etc. without people obsessively focused on success.	While successful people may have problems like anyone else, it is better to strive for success because at least those who are successful have resources to deal with problems.

Essay Task

Write a unified, coherent essay in which you evaluate multiple perspectives on whether success can be disastrous. In your essay, be sure to:

- analyze and evaluate the perspectives given

- state and develop your own perspective on the issue

- explain the relationship between your perspective and those given

Your perspective may be in full agreement with any of the others, in partial agreement, or wholly different. Whatever the case, support your ideas with logical reasoning and detailed, persuasive examples.

Understanding Ourselves

A better understanding of other people contributes to the development of moral virtues. We shall be both kinder and fairer in our treatment of others if we understand them better. Understanding ourselves and understanding others are connected, since as human beings we all have things in common. Do we need other people in order to understand ourselves?

Read and carefully consider these perspectives. Each suggests a particular way of thinking about knowing ourselves.

Perspective One	Perspective Two	Perspective Three
We are often surrounded by other people and outside influences. The best way to truly know oneself is through solitary reflection.	We get to know who we are and who we want to be by seeing what other people are like and what they value. Everything is relative and you need to see what other people are like to decide what kind of person you are.	People with strong personalities and senses of self can be surrounded by different people and still pay them no mind. These types of people can know themselves regardless of their surrounding.

Essay Task

Write a unified, coherent essay in which you evaluate multiple perspectives on whether we need other people in order to understand ourselves. In your essay, be sure to:

- analyze and evaluate the perspectives given

- state and develop your own perspective on the issue

- explain the relationship between your perspective and those given

Your perspective may be in full agreement with any of the others, in partial agreement, or wholly different. Whatever the case, support your ideas with logical reasoning and detailed, persuasive examples.

The Future

There is, of course, no legitimate branch of science that enables us to predict the future accurately. Yet the degree of change in the world is so overwhelming and so promising that the future, I believe, is far brighter than anyone has contemplated since the end of the Second World War. Is the world, in fact, changing for the better?

Read and carefully consider these perspectives. Each suggests a particular way of thinking about how the world is changing

Perspective One	Perspective Two	Perspective Three
Our continued development of technical knowledge and increasing power over the environment is actually a danger to ourselves. Without effective policy that addresses environmental concerns the future looks bleak.	The technology of ten years ago pales in comparison to what we have today. Since we will continue to develop technology at this rate, or even faster, the future will be an amazing place.	The world is becoming smaller and that is a good thing. As we have more of an ability to connect with and learn from people of different backgrounds there will be a newfound sense of tolerance and respect for other people.

Essay Task

Write a unified, coherent essay in which you evaluate multiple perspectives on whether the world has been changing for the better since the end of World War II. In your essay, be sure to:

- analyze and evaluate the perspectives given

- state and develop your own perspective on the issue

- explain the relationship between your perspective and those given

Your perspective may be in full agreement with any of the others, in partial agreement, or wholly different. Whatever the case, support your ideas with logical reasoning and detailed, persuasive examples.

The Role of Hardships

"Tough challenges reveal our strengths and weaknesses." This statement is certainly true; adversity helps us discover who we are. Hardships can often lead us to examine who we are and to questions what is important in life. In fact, people who have experienced seriously adverse events frequently report that they were positively changed by their negative experience. Do you think that ease does not challenge us and that we need adversity to help us discover who we are?

Read and carefully consider these perspectives. Each suggests a particular way of thinking about how adversity shapes who we are.

Perspective One	Perspective Two	Perspective Three
It is only by challenging ourselves that we can fully understand our own strengths and potential. When we make it through adversity we discover a deeper appreciation for our own abilities.	Adversity has the potential to scar us in a way that makes us afraid to explore or try new things. Intense trauma can paralyze us.	Adversity takes different forms for different people. Simply learning what is hard for you is part of discovering who you are.

Essay Task

Write a unified, coherent essay in which you evaluate multiple perspectives on whether we need adversity to discover who we are. In your essay, be sure to:

- analyze and evaluate the perspectives given

- state and develop your own perspective on the issue

- explain the relationship between your perspective and those given

Your perspective may be in full agreement with any of the others, in partial agreement, or wholly different. Whatever the case, support your ideas with logical reasoning and detailed, persuasive examples.

Heroism

Traditionally the term "heroism" has been applied to those who have braved physical danger to defend a cause or to protect others. But one of the most feared dangers people face is that of disapproval by their family, peers, or community. Sometimes acting courageously requires someone to speak out at the risk of such rejection. We should consider those who do so true heroes. Should heroes be defined as people who say that they think when we ourselves lack the courage to say it?

Read and carefully consider these perspectives. Each suggests a particular way of thinking about heroism and speech.

Perspective One	Perspective Two	Perspective Three
Words are not as powerful as actions, and as such it makes sense that we reserve the label of "hero" for those who take action in the face of physical danger. Those who speak out may be valiant, but they are not heroes.	Social pressure is a much more coercive and psychologically damaging force than physical danger. Therefore, those who speak out and risk such alienation and social pressure are true heroes.	With the advent of the internet, it is now easy to find a like-minded audience for even the most unpopular opinion. In that sense, people who speak out and alienate themselves can always find a new community for support.

Essay Task

Write a unified, coherent essay in which you evaluate multiple perspectives on whether heroes should be defined as people who say what they think when we ourselves lack the courage to say it. In your essay, be sure to:

- analyze and evaluate the perspectives given

- state and develop your own perspective on the issue

- explain the relationship between your perspective and those given

Your perspective may be in full agreement with any of the others, in partial agreement, or wholly different. Whatever the case, support your ideas with logical reasoning and detailed, persuasive examples.

Majority Rule

We must seriously question the idea of majority rule. The majority grinned and jeered when Columbus said the world was round. The majority threw him in a dungeon for his discoveries. Where is the logic in the notion that the opinion held by a majority of people should have the power to influence our decisions?

Read and carefully consider these perspectives. Each suggests a particular way of thinking about majority rule.

Perspective One	Perspective Two	Perspective Three
Most people are not experts, so the only thing majority rule guarantees is that experts' voices are not heard among the crowd. It is easier to place your faith in a few educated people than to educate everyone.	Majority rule is the only system that assures that the greatest good is done for the greatest amount of people. If individuals or small groups of people make decisions they will hoard resources and power.	As access to information and education continues to improve with technology majority rule will only get better as a system for decision making.

Essay Task

Write a unified, coherent essay in which you evaluate multiple perspectives on whether the opinion held by a majority of people should influence our decisions. In your essay, be sure to:

- analyze and evaluate the perspectives given

- state and develop your own perspective on the issue

- explain the relationship between your perspective and those given

Your perspective may be in full agreement with any of the others, in partial agreement, or wholly different. Whatever the case, support your ideas with logical reasoning and detailed, persuasive examples.

Individualism

A colleague of the great scientist James Watson remarked that Watson was always "lounging around, arguing about problems instead of doing experiments." He concluded that, "There is more than one way of doing good science." It was Watson's form of idleness, the scientist went on, that allowed him to solve " the greatest of all biological problems: the discovery of the structure of DNA." It is a point worth remembering in a society overly concerned with efficiency. Do people accomplish more when they are allowed to do things in their own way?

Read and carefully consider these perspectives. Each suggests a particular way of thinking about efficiency and following established processes.

Perspective One	Perspective Two	Perspective Three
When we follow tried and true methods we are utilizing generations worth of information. Most people who don't follow these methods are simply wasting their time by spurning such a wealth of information.	By repeating what has already been done it is impossible to improve efficiency. People need to experiment in order to innovate.	Even if people are less efficient when doing things their own way, by taking ownership of the process those people are likely to be passionate and as a result work harder and get more done.

Essay Task

Write a unified, coherent essay in which you evaluate multiple perspectives on whether people accomplish more when they are allowed to do things in their own way. In your essay, be sure to:

- analyze and evaluate the perspectives given

- state and develop your own perspective on the issue

- explain the relationship between your perspective and those given

Your perspective may be in full agreement with any of the others, in partial agreement, or wholly different. Whatever the case, support your ideas with logical reasoning and detailed, persuasive examples.

Truth

There is an old saying: "A person with one watch knows what time it is; a person with two watches isn't so sure." In other words, a person who looks at an object or event from two different angles sees something different from each position. Moreover, two or more people looking at the same thing may each perceive something different. In other words, truth, like beauty, may lie in the eye of the beholder. Does truth change depending on how people look at things?

Read and carefully consider these perspectives. Each suggests a particular way of thinking about the concept of truth.

Perspective One	Perspective Two	Perspective Three
Truth is a concrete concept, and when an idea or fact is proven through reason there can only be one correct understanding of that concept. This is the foundation for math and science.	Truth is a matter of perception. Everyone has a different background and set of biases, which allows each person to perceive an equally valid truth.	Not only does truth change based on individual view points, but it also changes based on collective viewpoints. Our personal ideas about truth are greatly affected by what the people around us think.

Essay Task

Write a unified, coherent essay in which you evaluate multiple perspectives on whether truth changes depending on how people look at things. In your essay, be sure to:

- analyze and evaluate the perspectives given

- state and develop your own perspective on the issue

- explain the relationship between your perspective and those given

Your perspective may be in full agreement with any of the others, in partial agreement, or wholly different. Whatever the case, support your ideas with logical reasoning and detailed, persuasive examples.

Identity

A person does not simply "receive" his or her identity. Identity is much more than the name or features one is born with. True identity is something people must create for themselves by making choices that are significant and that require a courageous commitment in the face of challenges. Identity means having ideas and values that one lives by. Is identity something people are born with or given, or is it something people create for themselves?

Read and carefully consider these perspectives. Each suggests a particular way of thinking about efficiency and following established processes.

Perspective One	Perspective Two	Perspective Three
We are living in an unprecedented age of individuality. As such, the only way to form an identity is to actively make decisions about what we value and adopt as our own.	Our identity is very closely tied with our emotional outlook and unique set of abilities, two things that we are more or less born with. For example, an artist cannot identify as an artist without the innate ability to create.	It takes a village to raise a child. As a result, someone's identity is often a product of the community in which that person was raised.

Essay Task

Write a unified, coherent essay in which you evaluate multiple perspectives on whether identity is something people are born with or soemthing people create for themselves. In your essay, be sure to:

- analyze and evaluate the perspectives given

- state and develop your own perspective on the issue

- explain the relationship between your perspective and those given

Your perspective may be in full agreement with any of the others, in partial agreement, or wholly different. Whatever the case, support your ideas with logical reasoning and detailed, persuasive examples.

2019-1